DEISM IN EIGHTEENTH CENTURY
AMERICA

DEISM IN EIGHTEENTH CENTURY AMERICA

BY

HERBERT M. MORAIS, Ph.D.

New York

RUSSELL & RUSSELL

1960

COPYRIGHT, 1934, BY
COLUMBIA UNIVERSITY PRESS
PUBLISHED, 1960, BY
RUSSELL & RUSSELL, INC.
L. C. CATALOG CARD NO.: 60 - 8198

PRINTED IN THE UNITED STATES OF AMERICA

To
MY PARENTS

" . . . Some American historian ought to re-relate to the world the full extent of [the] remarkable spread of skepticism in the eighteenth century . . . "

—JOSEPH MCCABE

" . . . [The] story of religious and philosophical thought in the eighteenth century is the story of the rising tide of deism, of the receding waves of orthodoxy . . . "

—HOWARD M. JONES

PREFACE

ALTHOUGH deism was the axis about which the religious thought of eighteenth-century America revolved, studies dealing with it have been few. Interest in the subject, however, seems to be growing; in fact, only a few months ago, an excellent work covering the rise of an organized deistic movement appeared. In his *Republican Religion, The American Revolution and the Cult of Reason* (1933), Koch shows how the formation of deistic clubs, lectureships and newspapers made possible the popularization of deism. Interested especially in this phase of the deistic tendency, he does not concern himself with deistic speculation as such, with its origins, European background and relation to other types of rationalistic expression. The present writer, however, emphasizes these points as well as the development of an organized deism. In addition to these subjects, he points out the connection of the deistic trend with the French and Indian War, Freemasonry and the infiltration of French culture. The religious views of the signers of the Declaration of Independence, of other Revolutionary War figures and of prominent Republican and Federalist leaders are examined in order to determine how far these men traveled along the road of skepticism. Circumstances have forced the author to confine most of his discussion to deism in the North; he has, however, included some material on other sections and is indebted for suggestions in this connection to Professors H. M. Jones of the University of Michigan and J. G. de R. Hamilton of the University of North Carolina.

7

The author has set himself the task of defining the deistic movement in the light of its eighteenth-century environment, of giving a general picture of its rise, progress and decline and of interpreting its tenor in terms of its class support. To understand deism more clearly the writer has distinguished it from atheism and Christian rationalism, has noted its connection with anti-clericalism and has examined its development in Europe. Eighteenth-century deism accepted the sufficiency of natural (rational) religion and implicitly or explicitly rejected the need or truth of divine revelation. The author has sought not only to define deism but also to trace its progress from 1713 to 1805. A number of considerations led him to select 1713 as the proper starting-point for his study; in that year the first work on deism published by an American, Cotton Mather's *Reasonable Religion,* appeared; one year later, the first great collection of rationalistic works was sent to America. The year 1805 was regarded as a fitting close because in that year Elihu Palmer, responsible for the organization of a militant deistic movement, died. Moreover, by 1805, the second Great Awakening had run its course and had succeeded in making the country safe for Christianity. From pamphlets, sermons, diaries, travelers' accounts, library catalogues, and especially periodicals, information was secured to show the advent of deism in colonial America, the extent of its influence on the eve of the Revolution, its growing militancy after 1783, its spread from the intelligentsia to the masses, and its temporary collapse in early nineteenth-century America.

Lastly, the effort is made to interpret deism in the light of its class support. During most of the eighteenth century, deistic speculation circulated almost exclusively among " rich and well-born " liberals who used it for the purpose of overthrowing such vestiges of the old regime as the union of church and state. The upper classes, however, did not desire to destroy " religion " and therefore they minimized the anti-Christian implications of the deistic philosophy. When Palmer and his associates initiated an organized movement emphasizing these inferences and carrying them to the masses, deistically-inclined planters and " substantial " merchants generally refused to support the tendency. Stripped of its chief source of financial and intellectual backing and faced by a determined and well-organized evangelical Christianity, the deism of Palmer was doomed to failure. Yet, the deistic movement did not wholly disappear; in fact, from 1825 to 1835, it again came to the front and this time its denunciation of Christianity was outspoken and bitter. Its anti-Christian inclinations were grounded in the fact that its advocates were Owenite socialists who were convinced that one of the ways to eliminate the " evils " of the system of private property was to free the people from " the opium of religion." In another work, the author intends to show how deism was moulded during the early nineteenth century to suit the revolutionary aspirations of the advance guard of workingclass discontent.

The writer heartily welcomes this opportunity to acknowledge his many and varied obligations to others who have aided him; to Professor Evarts B. Greene, of the Department of History, Columbia University, for his patience, scholarly attitude, and stimulating direction; to Professor Herbert W. Schneider, of the Department of Philosophy, Columbia University, for his encouragement and expert criticism; to Mr. Solomon Bloom, his colleague in the Department of History, Brooklyn College, for his correction of the manuscript and for his many enlightening suggestions; to Professor Holland Thompson, of the Department of History, of the City College of New York, for the impetus given to this study and for his helpful literary hints; to Professor J. Salwyn Schapiro, of the same institution, and to Professor John Herman Randall, Jr., Department of Philosophy, Columbia University, for their suggestions on European deism; to Professor A. G. Fradenburgh, head of the Department of History, Brooklyn College, for his careful reading of various parts of the book; and to the Misses Lillian Morais and Dorothy Neugeborn for their patience in typing and retyping the manuscript. Whatever good points the work may have are due in a large measure to the constructive criticisms of these men and women; whatever faults the book may have are my own.

BROOKLYN COLLEGE,
DECEMBER, 1933.

CONTENTS

CHAPTER I

General Character of the Deistic Movement With Particular Reference to America

Deism in America shared the cautious and non-revolutionary temper of eighteenth-century liberalism of which it was an integral part. Although a few of its bolder spirits achieved some contemporary notoriety for their militant attack upon revealed Christianity, most of the deistic champions were willing to leave the question of divine revelation alone. Their apparent lack of gusto may be explained in one of two ways. In the first place, these men, caught up by the intellectual currents of their age, were swept into an acceptance of deism without fully appreciating its implications. Consequently, many of them—Hawley, a Northampton lawyer, Bliss, a New England clergyman and Edmund and John Randolph, prominent Virginian statesmen—eventually retraced their steps and returned to the Christian fold.

Secondly, it required courage to take up the crusade against revealed Christianity; it meant the loss of social respectability. To speak pretty nothings was one thing; to court martyrdom for one's views was quite another. Not that these militant deists were hanged or burned or broken on the wheel: no, this was the Enlightened Age of Reason and Progress and not the Dark Ages. Hence, little boys were told to stick out their tongues at these undesirables, while their more civilized elders were cautioned to shun them. Ethan Allen, hero of Ticonderoga and author of the first real anti-Christian work in America, became in his day " a vile and impious wretch " destined to burn eternally; Thomas Paine, the man who, as Jefferson wrote, " steadily labored " to secure

13

American freedom, achieved the dubious reputation of being an "atheist" despite his explicit assertion "I believe in one God and no more . . ."; while Elihu Palmer, the most aggressive of native-born deists, was described as "superficial, vain and affectatious." Social disapproval was expressed in subtler forms than those of vituperation. Militant champions of the deistic cause were concretely taught that deism did not pay. Isaac Hall, of Philadelphia, an agent for Palmer's deistic newspaper, the *Prospect,* was, according to rumor, refused the lease of a municipal wharf because of his membership in the "Tom Paine crowd." [1]

Moreover, another consideration made possible the victory of prudence over ardor. An attack upon the Christian system of faith and morals might be accompanied by undesirable social consequences. Such an eventuality was far from being relished by most of these liberal gentlemen. Drawn as they were from the "rich and the well-born", they did not oppose the spread of deism among the upper classes; they did, however, fear its dissemination among the masses. One contemporary clergyman, although condemning the anti-Christian inclinations of Hume, Bolingbroke and Gibbon, was nevertheless quite willing to praise them for the "good sense" they showed in confining their observations to "the more polished classes of the community. . . ." [2] Another eighteenth-century liberal was even more explicit; the upper classes used the "superstitions" of Christianity to enslave the masses. In a letter to the Editor of *The Temple of Reason* for November 27, 1802, "A Rich Deist" wrote,

Very few rich men; or, at least men in the higher grades of society, and who receive a liberal education, care anything about

[1] Koch, *Republican Religion, The American Revolution and The Cult of Reason* (New York, 1933), p. 144.

[2] From a sermon by Robert Hall on Modern Infidelity Considered with respect to its Influence on Society quoted *ibid.,* p. 75.

the Christian religion. They cast off the yoke of superstition themselves; yet, for the sake of finding obedient servants, they would continue to impose it on the poor.

Thus, the anti-Christian tendency of militant deistic ideology was too dangerous for the peace of society. It concealed tons of social dynamite which, if set off, would destroy not only organized religion but the social order.

Most American deists, therefore, contented themselves with the innocuous common-sense truths of "the pure and simple Religion of Nature" with its basic premise of a First Cause, its acceptance of a future state and its emphasis upon virtuous living. This threefold creed, however, was not entirely monopolized by the "Deistic Knights of the goose-quill"; it was also accepted by the rationalistic clergy of the age, Gay, Briant and Bentley in Congregational surroundings and Johnson and Smith in Anglican circles. Yet, these ministers held that the authoritative basis of natural religion did not rest in reason alone but also depended upon the Christian revelation which clarified its precepts and added weight to its teachings. So long as liberals were pleased to express their approval of the religion of nature, all went well. But the moment they neglected to mention the necessity of the Bible as an aid to "the new faith", or, even worse, the moment they denied openly the need or truth of the Scriptures, the die was cast and the battle begun.

For the most part, however, the conflict was neither exciting nor dramatic because of the general lukewarmness of American deism which criticized Christianity in the guarded phraseology of the would-be reformer rather than of the determined destroyer. Desiring to make the Christian religion conform more fully with the intellectual currents of rationalistic science, most deists assiduously presented Jesus to their contemporaries as the first great deistic preacher, a man who, in the words of Jefferson, endeavored to recall the

Hebrews "to the principles of a pure deism, . . . to reform their moral doctrines to the standards of reason, justice and philanthropy, and to inculcate a belief in a future state. . . ." [3] Other exponents of the deistic philosophy were even bolder; they claimed that the simple carpenter of Nazareth was a "moral" deist who, like Paine, Volney and Palmer, desired men to love God and their neighbors. [4] According to the deists, the followers of Jesus lost sight of his teachings to the extent of replacing them with rituals, creeds and churches. Consequently, the religion of the Gospels was in need of redemption and in response to the necessity, deistic saviors appeared on the scene who proposed to strip Christianity of its "useless" accretions. By doing away with these additions, these deists hoped to see the restoration of the "pure and simple teachings" of Jesus, which teachings were "the best the World ever saw or is likely to see. . . ." [5] Since these sage precepts could be discovered by reason, all men could share them.

Prior to 1784, the American deistic movement made no real effort to examine openly and critically "the revealed word of God." During the colonial period, freethinkers were satisfied with the harmless approach of setting forth the tenets of natural religion without seeking an authoritative basis for them in the Bible. They made no attempt to popularize their views; rather than air their observations they confined them to letters and diaries. Fearful of social ostracism, many of the early disciples of deism—Hawley, Bliss and John Adams—sooner or later disavowed their "youthful fancies". The introduction of English ration-

[3] T. Jefferson, *Writings*, ed. Ford (New York, 1892), vol. viii, p. 224 (footnote).

[4] *Temple of Reason*, vol. i, p. 9. See issues for November 8, 15, and 22, 1800.

[5] B. Franklin, *Writings*, ed. Smyth (New York, 1905-7), vol. x, p. 84.

alistic works, the cosmic philosophy of Newton, the empirical psychology of Locke, the appearance of a liberal theological movement and some anti-clerical feeling prepared the way for the advent of deistic speculation in colonial America. Its progress during the provincial period was, however, very slow; in fact, up to 1776, deism was still an aristocratic cult confined to a few intellectuals residing in relatively large towns. In these cities as well as in the interior, it was regarded with a great deal of suspicion and hostility. Yet, in spite of its unpopularity, a large number of Revolutionary leaders either accepted it or came very close to doing so. Of the fifty-six delegates who signed the Declaration of Independence, the religious opinions of twenty were ascertained. Of these, three were deists, Jefferson, Franklin and Hopkins; two were veering towards deism, John Adams and Wythe; four, Robert Treat Paine, Bartlett, Rush and Thornton, entertained liberal, though not deistic, views; while the remaining eleven were orthodox in their principles. The same diversity of religious opinions which characterized the signers of the immortal Declaration prevailed among others who played an important role in the revolutionary struggle. Willie Jones of North Carolina, member of the Continental Congress, Edmund Randolph, prominent Virginian statesman, Ethan Allen, military leader and Thomas Paine, author of *Common Sense,* rejected either implicitly or explicitly the Christian revelation, while George Washington, James Madison and George Mason came dangerously close to doing the same thing. On the other hand, men like Samuel Adams, Patrick Henry and Henry Laurens were, in spite of their political liberalism, conservatives in religion.[6]

During the Revolutionary era, deism became somewhat bolder in tone; in 1784, in his ponderous and repetitious *Reason, the Only Oracle of Man,* Allen rejected revealed

6 See chapter iv, pp. 92-8, 100-3, 104-5, 113-8; chapter v, pp. 120-6, 141-2.

religion in general and Christianity in particular. Although not typical of the American climate of deistic opinion, he nevertheless represented a significant swing to the left, a swing stimulated by the rising anti-clerical spirit of the age. At the close of the Revolutionary War, established churches and religious discriminations existed in several American states. To the advance guard of deistic liberalism, liberty meant freedom not only from English but also from ecclesiastical interference. The forced payment of taxes to an established church and compulsory adherence to its dogmas were considered as derogatory to the nature of man as well as useless and pernicious to social welfare. According to the deists, it mattered little whether all men accepted transubstantiation or consubstantiation, infant or adult baptism, so long as they obeyed the laws of the land. Good citizenship based on freedom was of greater value to society than blind acceptance of a formulated creed which too often deluded its adherents. On the other hand, a general agreement as to dogmas was, they thought, necessary to the continuance in power of an established church which, whether Protestant or Catholic, would use the civil machinery to stamp out opposition. In the encouragement of fanaticism, the clergy, who were supported by forced contributions drawn from public funds subscribed to by believers and non-believers, were ever ready to " furnish their quota of imps " and transform Biblical phrases into weapons for killing. To the deistic liberal, the bloody struggles, which so often disgraced the pages of Christian history, could only be avoided in the future if clerical dogmatism were destroyed.

In order to put an end to ecclesiastical interference the deists sought to undermine priestly pretentions to authority. In the last analysis, these rested upon an acceptance of the Bible as a divine document. American deists might therefore be expected to attack the Scriptural revelation explicitly

and boldly; but, during this period, with the exception of
Allen, they did not. So vigorous was Allen's reaction
against the priesthood that he declared himself to be no
Christian " except as infant baptism made [him] so. . . ."
Driven by the same anti-clerical spirit, the deistic Charles Lee,
a general under Washington, directed his heirs not to bury
his remains in a church or churchyard, while John Randolph
of Virginia viewed with pleasure any victory of the Crescent
over the Cross. Likewise Willie Jones, prominent Revolutionary leader of North Carolina, stated in his will that he
wanted no priest to insult his body by saying anything over
it. Yet, the North Carolinian did not go so far as to openly
reject revealed religion. On the whole, his position was
similar to that of his friend, Jefferson, who played a leading
role in the disestablishment of the Anglican Church in Virginia. Like most American deists, the author of the Declaration of Independence was satisfied with drawing a nice
distinction between the religion of the Gospels and that of
the priests. He proposed to destroy the latter in order to
restore the simple teachings of Jesus, which he thought, were
essentially deistic. By this means, the dawn of the Enlightened Age of Natural Religion would begin.

Although anti-clericalism was prevalent during the Revolutionary era, it was not strong enough to produce an aggressive deistic tendency. This was postponed until after
1793 and was brought about by the activities of the ministry
which forced more radical deistic liberals to invade the
sacred domain of the Biblical revelation. Circumstances
moved Paine and Palmer, the two outstanding deistic critics
of Christianity in America, to throw caution to the winds.
During the French Revolution, Paine felt that the clergy of
France was allied with the descredited monarchical forces
of reaction. In order to overthrow the alliance of throne
and altar and to preserve republican and liberal principles, he

determined to destroy the priesthood by putting an end to the source of its authority—the Scriptural revelation. The growth of atheism, which appeared to him to threaten the existence of the only true religion, deism, was another consideration motivating the Anglo-American radical to attack the divine origin of the Scriptures. In his view, disbelief in God and a future state was due to the disgust men felt for the fanatical and reactionary tendencies of the clerical party. Thus, to save deism from atheism and republicanism from despotism, the defender of the Rights of Man published his *Age of Reason* (1794). He had contemplated the writing of such a destructive work for a long time but, true to the cautious temper of eighteenth-century liberalism, he had hesitated to do so. At a very early age, Paine came to doubt the validity of the Christian revelation but was reluctant to develop publicly the destructive implications of the deistic philosophy. Although he informed John Adams in 1776 that he intended to publish a work against the Old Testament, he failed to do so. Some ten years later, Franklin, in a letter believed to have been addressed to Paine, prudently advised him to give up this project and " display his Talents of reasoning upon a less hazardous subject and thereby obtain a Rank with our distinguish'd Authors. . . ." [7]   It was not

---

[7] B. Franklin, *Writings*, ed. Smyth, vol. ix, p. 521. That this letter might have been written to Paine appears probable for we know that the Anglo-American intended to compose a deistic tract in 1776 and that he informed John Adams of his intentions. What was to prevent him from entertaining similar designs in 1786 and telling them to his friend Franklin who, in line with his prudent habits, would advise against the publication of any such work? That the above letter was written to Paine to stop him from writing his *Age of Reason* (as was later contended) does not seem likely. Joseph Lewis, in his *Franklin the Freethinker*, attempts to show that this was not the case. He argues that *The Age of Reason* was published a number of years after the above letter was sent and that it was written, according to Paine, without any one being consulted.

until he was almost sixty and in the shadow of the guillotine that the Anglo-American decided to modify his life-long resolve of never dishonoring religion nor of ridiculing " any denomination whatsoever."

Circumstances likewise made Elihu Palmer, teacher, minister and lawyer, denounce publicly the Christian religion. Forced to give up his pulpit in a Philadelphia Baptist Church because of heterodox views, prevented from holding meetings of his own because of clerical hostility, the blind preacher was ready in 1793 to accept the challenge of the French Revolution. Like Paine, this Dartmouth graduate proposed to save liberalism by fighting what seemed to him to be its bitterest opponent—the clergy. From 1793 onward, Congregational ministers of New England allied themselves with Federalistic conservatism and in order to stem the rising tide of democratic ideas, they cast aspersions upon the French Revolution and its principles of Liberty and Equality. To save these principles, Palmer, armed with that powerful engine of destruction, *The Age of Reason,* determined to put an end to the clergy by destroying belief in revealed religion. In short, the clerical forces of Old France and New England obliged more radical deistic liberals to attack what Paine was pleased to call

the Christian system of faith, including in it the whimsical account of the creation, the strange story of Eve, the snake and the apple; the ambiguous idea of a man-god; the corporeal idea of the death of a god; the mythological idea of a family of gods, and the Christian system of arithmetic that three is one and one is three. . . .[8]

The militant anti-Christian approach of Paine and Palmer, however, was not pursued by all deistic liberals. Most of them adopted the cautious procedure of Freneau and Jeffer-

[8] T. Paine, *Age of Reason* (New York, no date), pt. i, p. 57.

son who, while bitterly castigating the clergy, did not openly reject revealed religion. Likewise it would be misleading to assume that all of those who marched under the banners of Jeffersonian republicanism and equalitarianism were even moderate deists. In western Pennsylvania, Scotch-Irish Presbyterians, although active in the radical politics of their state, were conservatives in religion. William Findley and John Smilie, popular Republican leaders, represented the religious conservatism of their constituents; on one occasion, Findley and his associates were quite willing to bolt their party rather than accept a gubernatorial candidate reputed to be a member of the " Tom Paine crowd ". In New England, God-fearing Baptists and Methodists were usually Jeffersonians but at the same time were the backbone of the evangelical movement which more than anything else was responsible for the decline of deism. Likewise Republican leadership was not drawn exclusively from deistic ranks; Barlow and Sullivan entertained liberal, though not deistic, views, while Samuel Adams was so firm a believer in the Christian revelation that he observed with sorrow Paine's attempt to convert good American citizens to " so bad a cause " as deism. Conversely, not all Federalist leaders were religious conservatives; Timothy Pickering, Josiah Quincy and John Adams of Massachusetts held Unitarian views, while William Davie of North Carolina was a deist and Charles Cotesworth Pinckney of South Carolina was accused of being one.

Yet, because of the noisy aggressiveness of " Tom Paine and his infidels " and the attention bestowed upon them by a thoroughly frightened clergy, militant deism attracted an attention out of proportion to its actual influence. Convinced that the best defense was a good offense, it trained its siege guns of criticism upon the citadel of revealed Christianity. Deistic societies and newspapers were used at the turn of the century to demolish the Biblical revelation. Of these two agencies, the former were by far more important since serving at first as cells of resistance, they were later to be employed as cells of organization for the establishment of " the new faith ". They distributed deistic works free of charge, initiated discussions, collected money and instructed their members to turn their dogs upon unhappy Christian ministers. New York, Philadelphia, Newburgh, Baltimore and the Genesee River country in western New York State had such societies. Freethinking newspapers were also established to spread " the glad tidings of a new day "; *The Temple of Reason* (1800-1803), published in New York and Philadelphia, was designed to show the purity and soundness of deistic principles, while *The Prospect, or View of the Moral World* (1803-1805), printed in New York, proposed to investigate fully the divine nature of Christianity. Back of these two agencies of propaganda was Elihu Palmer who offered to do for natural religion what St. Paul had already done for Christianity. From Newburgh to Atlanta, this apostle of missionary deism addressed enthusiastic audiences, the size of which varied, as far as accounts go, in direct ratio to the sympathies of his reporters. Incapable of making anyone weary " within the sound of his voice " he was a brilliant speaker, and, although he vigorously assailed the Christian religion, his attack was according to one authority,[9] even less daring than that of his New York co-worker, John Foster.

Through the publication of popularized deistic tracts and the formation of Freethinking societies, newspapers and lectureships, the deism of Paine made its way among students, planters, doctors, teachers, merchants and farmers. Its evident popularity caused consternation among the faithful who were so alarmed that they felt only a miracle could save

[9] Francis, *New York during the last Half Century* (New York, 1857), p. 92.

their religion. This was reflected in an appeal made by the New York Missionary Society in 1798. Addressed to all those who "love our Lord Jesus Christ in sincerity", the plea read,

. . . Infidelity abounds. It hath assumed an imperious air, and glories in the expectation of a speedy extermination of the religion of Jesus. To confound its vain hopes, we are called upon to shew that the Spirit of Christ continues to animate his body . . . [The] Lord is about to build up Zion, and to appear in his glory. Amen. Even so: come Lord Jesus! [10]

Verily, the faithful were standing at Armageddon and battling for the Lord. They conducted their defense of Christianity along two fronts, one rational and the other emotional. The former was reflected in the appearance of apologetic works intended especially to show the irrationality of Paine's contentions. Alongside of this rational tendency, there emerged an evangelical movement whose message appealed more readily to the people since it was addressed to their hearts and not to their minds. In its wake came missionary agencies, orthodox magazines, theological seminaries, Bible societies and Sunday Schools, all of which proved too powerful for the poorly organized deism of the militant forces. Yet, the deistic movement made too much of an impression to disappear entirely; it merged into the Higher Criticism of the nineteenth century and even lives on today in the discourses of modernistic clergymen and the harangues of atheistic speakers.

English deism was marked by the same cautious approach and internal division as the American tendency. Like most of their co-workers in the new Republic, English deists contented themselves with setting forth the sufficiency of natural

[10] *The Theological Magazine*, June, July, and August 1798, vol. iii, pp. 267, 270.

religion and the consequent lack of necessity for revealed
" truths ". Tindal and Chubb identified the tenets of the
religion of nature with the simple teachings of Christ which
they hoped " to restore ". Yet, a few champions of English
deism strayed from the straight and narrow path and, like
Collins and Woolston, openly denounced Christianity. For
this they were bitterly condemned; Woolston, who portrayed
Jesus as an impostor, sorcerer and magician, was fined and
imprisoned, an act which constituted a slight miscarriage of
the much-vaunted British spirit of tolerance. These men
were moved to express themselves with such boldness because
of their intense dislike for organized Christianity with its
rituals, creeds and clergy. This anti-clerical feeling, however, was not strong enough in England to produce a widespread militant deism. The established Church of England
pursued a liberal latitudinarian policy which, as a mode of
thought, tended to promote deism by emphasizing rational
religion and minimizing revelation.

Whereas a vigorous anti-clericalism was for the most part
lacking in eighteenth-century America and England, that
was not the case in France and, consequently, in that country
the destructive implications of the deistic philosophy were
most fully developed. Here, the Catholic Church, as a great
landholder and recipient of privileges, was closely associated
with the rapidly decaying feudal order. Abuses were prevalent within the Church and liberal philosophers seized upon
these to strike at the mighty Gallican establishment in the
hope of reforming the old regime. They viewed with envy
and alarm the political power exercised by the Jesuit order,
which power they thought was being used to advance bigotry
and intolerance. They became convinced that this was the
case when the Protestant Calas was tortured to death (1761)
and when, four years later, the headless body of a sixteen-
year old boy, La Barre, was cast into the flames on the ground

that he had mutilated crucifixes. It was then, and only then, that Voltaire in the name of Reason and Liberty called upon his friends, Diderot, D'Alembert and others, "to destroy the infamy" by discrediting the source of clerical power—the Bible. Although the Church opposed external divergences of opinion even to the extent of stamping them out, she was conveniently oblivious to latitudinarian views within her ranks where a goodly number of deistic Abbé Gaimes and relatively few atheistic Abbé Mesliers could be found.

Yet, French freethinkers, like Voltaire, if left to themselves, might never have fought Christianity. The logic of events more than personal convictions forced the sage of Ferney to take up the battle. The fiery Frenchman, who came in contact with deism during his English visit (1726-1729), was led to doubt the validity of the Christian revelation at a rather early age but really made no serious attack on it until he was seventy and then only because of clerical activities in reference to the Calas incident. In his *Treatise on Toleration,* issued at this time, he let the cat out of the bag by stating that he would have borne with the absurd dogmas of the Church had she tolerated differences of opinion; but since she refused to do so the tacit understanding between them was at an end. In Voltaire's view clerical intolerance led to bloodshed, and therefore if peace within society were to be preserved, ecclesiastical power had to be overthrown by exposing Christianity's assumption of divine origin.

Although Voltaire remained a deist throughout his life, when he finished saying what God was not, the Supreme Being had few positive attributes left. Thus, it was an easy matter for his more radical associates to deny God and a future state; in short, militant deism in France led straight to atheism. This was more than Voltaire had bargained for; in spite of his professed boldness, he refused to take the next logical step in this battle of negations. True to his deistic heritage, he sought to combat the " false " reason of atheism with the " right " reason of deism. His rationalistic arguments, defending the existence of God, were derived from design and necessity. To Voltaire, the harmonious order of nature proclaimed the presence of a benevolent, just and intelligent Maker who had created the universe and had given it the initial impetus. As to the contention that the world presented a clear picture of its having been designed by an intelligent Architect, eighteenth-century skeptics held that even if this argument were true, it proved only the existence of a Being superior to man, whose workmanship might be faulty in comparison with that of other worlds. In opposition to Voltaire's argument that an independent and external Being was needed to set the heavenly bodies in motion, the Baron d'Holbach contended that such a moving force was inherent in nature itself. Holbach further maintained that the tendency of deism to ascribe fixed attributes to God, as benevolence, justice and intelligence, was useless because no one could have definite ideas about a Being who did not act upon the senses. Moreover, such characterizations were not only futile but pernicious since they sought to perpetuate ignorance under the guise of knowledge.

Yet, despite these atheistic contentions, Voltaire and his deistic friends felt that they still held a trump in their hand of tricks—the ace of social utility. Most people, they argued were virtuous because they hoped to be rewarded, or feared to be punished, in a future life, a consideration conducive to social welfare. The future state obviously pre-supposed the existence of a just and wise Deity who dispensed with fine precision individual rewards and punishments. Remove the idea of God and you destroy a belief in an after-life and with it a potent check upon the mob. This was behind Voltaire's famous remark, " If God did not exist it would be necessary to invent him ". On the other hand, the atheists contended that men could be taught to do good and avoid evil through channels other than those of fear. They proposed a system of education and legislation designed to inculcate virtue; their chief, d'Holbach, significantly observed that if men were bad, they were made so and not born so.

Thus, whether in Europe or America, deism retained in the end the essentially cautious temper of eighteenth-century liberalism. In France, where its negations were most fully developed, atheism resulted. Confronted with so dangerous "an enemy to social welfare ", French deists, led by their chief, Voltaire, prudently called a halt to the vagaries of reason and finished by accepting God and a future state. In America, where the attack upon revealed Christianity was not as pronounced because of a relatively less intense anti-clericalism, most deistic advocates judiciously rendered lip-service to the cause of natural religion without explicitly assailing the divine origin of the Biblical revelation. When a few bolder spirits did so, they were bitterly assailed by the faithful. In the last analysis, then, deism proved too conservative and compromising for the atheist and yet, in its destructive phase, too radical and unyielding for the Christian; thus it eventually passed into the limbo of unfortunate causes attempting to steer a middle course. For the reader to understand the intellectual source of the American deistic movement as well as its direction relative to similar tendencies the world over, it is essential to examine its European background.

CHAPTER II

EUROPEAN BACKGROUND

ONE factor in the rise of deism during the colonial period was the importation of English rationalistic works. In the early eighteenth century, Jeremiah Dummer, an agent of the Connecticut colony, sent over to America seven hundred books, donated by Elihu Yale, Isaac Newton and others, which formed the basis for the Yale library. Among these volumes were some of the writings of Shaftesbury, a deist, and Tillotson, a believer in both rationalistic natural religion and revelation. During the same period, Thomas Hollis, a liberal Baptist in England, gave a large collection of writings to Harvard College among which were many tracts on religion. Similarly English theological works, especially those of Tillotson, were transported to Virginia for the benefit of the Anglican clergy of that colony. Before his death (1751), James Logan of Philadelphia, statesman, scholar and scientist, collected from two to three thousand books, most of which he had purchased in England and all of which he left to his native city.[1] While English rationalistic works were not widely circulated, it is evident that they found readers. The literary contributions of such defenders of the faith as Tillotson, Locke, Clarke and Cheyne as well as those of English deists, Herbert, Blount, Wollaston, Shaftesbury, Collins and Bolingbroke, were frequently re-

---

[1] Wright, *Literary Culture in Early New England* (New Haven, 1920), p. 186; Schneider, *The Puritan Mind* (New York, 1930), pp. 162, 193; Meade, *Old Churches, etc.* (Philadelphia, 1861), pp. 354-5; and Lamberton, *Colonial Libraries of Pennsylvania* (Pennsylvania Magazine of History and Biography, vol. 42, no. 3 [1918], pp. 210-11).

ferred to in colonial periodicals, books, sermons and library catalogues.[2]   Obviously these works promoted the growth of deism; on the one hand, the importation of English deistic books taught colonial freethinkers the principles of the new movement, while, on the other, the introduction of the writings of the rationalistic school of English theology, which subscribed to natural religion and the Christian revelation, gave American readers like Franklin an easy opportunity to accept the first and reject the second.

The lack of a vigorous anti-clericalism as well as common cultural ties caused colonial deists to adopt the generally mild tenor of the English movement.   Most of the advocates of

[2] For references to these men see *The American Magazine*, August, 1744, November, 1744 and February, 1745; T. Clap, *Essay on the Nature, etc.* (New Haven, 1765), pp. 31, 33; J. Edwards, *Works,* ed. S. L. Dwight (New York, 1830), vol. ii, p. 84; E. Gay, *Natural Religion, As Distinguish'd from Revealed* (Boston, 1759), pp. 13-5; S. Johnson, *Letter from Aristocles to Authades* (Boston, 1745), pp. 7, 13, 19; *Introduction to the Study of Philosophy* (New London, 1743), pp. 19, 28-9; W. Smith, *Discourses* (London, 1762), p. 43 (Appendix); W. Livingston, *Philosophical Solitude* (New York, 1747), p. 35; J. Adams, *Works,* ed. C. F. Adams (Boston, 1850), vol. ii, pp. 23, 105 and B. Franklin, *Writings,* ed. Smyth (New York, 1905-7), vol. x, p. 148.   For the works of Tillotson see *Harvard Catalogue,* 1725 (in Wright, *op. cit.,* p. 294), *Yale Catalogue* (Clap, *A Catalogue of the Library of Yale College in New Haven* [New London, 1743], pp. 27, 34), *Library Company of Philadelphia* (Philadelphia, 1764), p. 5, Byrd, *Writings,* ed. Bassett (New York, 1901), p. 427, and Knox, *Catalogue* (Boston, 1773).   For Locke consult Byrd, *op. cit.,* p. 442, *Harvard Catalogue* (in Wright, *op. cit.,* p. 294) and *Library Company of Philadelphia,* p. 5.   For Clarke and Cheyne see *Harvard Catalogue* (in Palfrey, *History of New England* [Boston, 1897], vol. i, p. 384, note), *Yale Catalogue* (in Clap, *op. cit.,* pp. 10, 22), Johnson, *Catalogue of my Library,* 1726 (MS.), *Library Company of Philadelphia,* p. 63 and Knox, *Catalogue,* p. 11.   For Herbert, Blount and Wollaston see *Harvard Catalogue* (in Palfrey, *op. cit.,* vol. i, p. 384, note), Byrd, *op. cit.,* p. 428), *Yale Catalogue* (Clap. *op. cit.,* p. 22), *Library Company of Philadelphia,* p. 34.   For Shaftesbury, Pope and Bolingbroke consult *Yale Catalogue* (Wright, *op. cit.,* p. 186 and Clap, *op. cit.,* p. 42), *Library Company of Philadelphia,* pp. 73, 91, 129 and Knox, *Catalogue,* pp. 7, 28.

the deistic philosophy in England contented themselves with setting forth the tenets of the religion of nature without seeking an authoritative foundation for them in the Biblical revelation. Only a few dared to reject explicitly the miracles and prophecies of Christ. From an historical viewpoint, English deism was an important link in a chain of thought starting from the Reformation. In place of the authority of the Catholic Church, the Protestants substituted that of the Bible and, during the century succeeding the Protestant Revolt, Hobbes and other thinkers insisted that the Scriptures be subjected to an historical and rational criticism. The deists went further and, as they thought, deeper. They asserted that the basis of authority was to be found in reason and in the rational beliefs, common to all men, to which it universally led. Among the first to adopt such a stand was Lord Herbert of Cherbury (1581-1648) who attempted to state what these universal principles were. In his work on the *Religion of the Gentiles with the Causes of their Errors,* he formulated five fundamental articles of faith. His creed consisted of a belief in (1) the existence of God; (2) His Worship; (3) the practice of virtue; (4) repentance of sin; and (5) a faith in immortality. Herbert held that these tenets were self-evident and were equally available to all ages and every country. This was due to the fact that they were based on the rational endowment of all men. Reason, too, was the test of the validity of all books professing to be revealed.[3] Similarly, Charles Blount (1654-1693), in his *Oracles of Reason,* written toward the close of the seventeenth century, was more interested in asserting the ethical basis of faith than in assailing Christianity. " . . . Our Religion ", he wrote, " must necessarily be this, to do good to [His] Creatures; for therein we concur with the will of

[3] Herbert of Cherbury, *Religion of the Gentiles, etc.* (London, 1705), pp. 3-4, 255, 257, 263, 268, 299-302, 327-8, 333.

God. . . ." Moreover, he was a firm believer in reason, "the greatest gift of the Deity". Deism was "a good manuring of a man's Conscience " and if sowed with Christianity, would " produce the most profitable Crop." [4]

The approach of Blount and Herbert, characteristic of seventeenth-century English deism, continued to mark the movement in the eighteenth. Toland, Tindal, Chubb and Wollaston sought to advance the cause of natural religion but made no real effort to examine the Christian revelation under the microscope of rationalistic science. Like Blount and Herbert, they were satisfied that the Scriptures were not necessary to establish the true principles of religion which could be determined by reason. Both Tindal and Chubb carefully identified deism with Christianity and pictured Jesus as the first great deistic preacher. Between the last decade of the seventeenth century and the middle of the eighteenth, only a few deists, notably Woolston and Collins, rejected this harmless approach and explicitly denied the truth of Biblical prophecies and miracles. The outstanding difference between the earlier deism of the seventeenth century and the later one of the eighteenth was that the latter was by far more fashionable. Its evident popularity was due to a variety of causes. The general acceptance after the " Glorious Revolution " of a policy of toleration, which afforded freethinkers an opportunity to express their views, was conducive to the spread of deism. Although Socinians and Catholics were denied the right to worship by the Toleration Act of 1689, this affected only a small minority. Moreover, the Press Licensing Act of 1662, which forbade the printing of heterdox books, was eventually allowed to lapse

---

[4] C. Blount, *Oracles of Reason* (London, 1693), pp. 92-3, 95. To the practice of virtue he added the two other tenets of the deistic creed, the existence of God and the immortality of the soul, *ibid.*, pp. 90-1, 122, 124-5.

during the reign of William III. Yet, because of the increased activity of deistic writers, a statute was passed in 1698 providing for the punishment of any person brought up in the Christian faith who published, taught or spoke any doctrines denying the Trinity, or the existence of God, or the divine authority of the Bible. Under the provisions of this act, deists, like Woolston and Annet, were imprisoned and the latter was also pilloried for " insulting language ".[5] Yet, the prosecution of these two men was exceptional, since the British ruling classes were generally tolerant towards the opponents of Christianity.

Another factor favorable to the spread of deism was the Latitudinarian movement which originated in an attempt to broaden the Anglican Church so as to admit to its communion a large proportion of Non-Conformists. Latitudinarianism, however, was more than a Church policy; it was a mode of thought which emphasized rational religion as a basis of agreement and frequently tended to minimize the importance of revelation. It was founded upon the two-fold conviction that the greatest possible freedom of discussion should prevail as to non-essentials, and that the basic principles of Christianity were few. Liberty of expression was advocated because it was believed that no one generation or church had fully attained divine truth. The net result of this rationalistic movement, in spite of the genuine piety of many of its leaders, was to stress a secular and rationalistic religious life at the expense of spiritual depth and fervour. Emphasizing reason and free inquiry, the Latitudinarians investi-

---

[5] Bury, *A History of Freedom of Thought* (New York, 1913), pp. 139-40; McGiffert, *Protestant Thought Before Kant* (New York, 1911), p. 192; Overton and Relton, *English Church from the Accession of George I to the End of the Eighteenth Century* (London, 1906), pp. 38-9; and Stephen, *English Thought in the Eighteenth Century* (New York, 1902), vol. i, p. 89.

gated the Bible in order to ascertain the basic tenets of Christianity as well as the divine authenticity of the Scriptural revelation.   They found the essential articles of the Christian religion to be the same as those of the religion of nature. Consequently, they unconsciously popularized the positive side of the deistic faith. Although resembling the deists in their advocacy of natural religion, the "Latitude men" differed from them in their acceptance of the validity of the Christian revelation.

John Tillotson (1630-1694), Archbishop of Canterbury, was representative of the moderate Latitudinarianism shared by many thoughtful and religious churchmen of the eighteenth century.   Although the deistical Collins asserted that Tillotson was the head of all freethinkers, the Anglican archbishop fought the deists with reasonable arguments.   His position was that of a rationalist who was ready to accept the tenets of natural religion but who held that these must be supplemented by the Christian revelation.   He defined the religion of nature as "obedience to Natural Law, and the performance of such duties as Natural Light, without any express and supernatural revelation, doth dictate to man. . . ." Its articles consisted of a belief in God, in the immortality of the soul and the practice of virtue.   Natural religion, the basis of revealed faith, needed the aid of the Christian revelation in order to strengthen its moral precepts.   To Tillotson, the divine origin of Christianity was attested by its fulfillment of the prophecies of the Old Testament, by its miracles and by its consistency with the nature of God.[6]   John Locke (1632-1704) adopted the same Latitudinarian views as did his contemporary, the Archbishop of Canterbury.   In his *Reasonableness of Christianity,* the apologist of the "Glorious Revolution" attempted to prove

[6] J. Tillotson, *Works* (London, 1717), vol. i, pp. 346, 350, 450-1, 616-22, 775; vol. ii, pp. 116, 119-26, 377, 527 *et seq.,* 575.

that the Christian religion was rational and yet divinely confirmed. Locke held that two things were necessary for salvation: " faith and repentance, that is, believing Jesus to be the Messiah, and a good life. . . ." This two-fold doctrine was the basis of the Christian system which was wholly consistent with reason, since, if a person attempted to live virtuously and believed in the divinity of Christ, allowances would be made for his imperfections. Moreover, Locke was convinced that the miracles performed by Jesus and his disciples proved the divine origin of Christianity.[7]

Similarly, Samuel Clarke (1675-1729), a close student of the Newtonian science and of the Scriptures, argued that the supernatural revelation of Christianity was required to aid natural religion; that it was in accord with man's notions concerning God; and that it was composed of rational doctrines. Moreover, he contended that the truth of Christianity was evidenced by the character of its founder, his fulfillment of the Hebraic prophecies, his performance of miracles, and the testimony of his apostles. Clarke maintained that the deistic attack upon revelation was essentially destructive in tendency and that atheism was its logical outcome.[8] George Cheyne (1671-1743), a doctor of medicine and a Fellow of the Royal Society, was another Latitudinarian who was read in colonial America. His *Philosophical Principles of Religion: Natural and Revealed* (1715) " though containing nothing great or original ", was " evidently the work of a zealous and pious man [whose] application of mathematics to theology [was] . . . very strange and fantastic. . . ."[9]

[7] J. Locke, *Reasonableness of Christianity* (no place or date given), pp. 19, 21-2, 40.

[8] S. Clarke, *A Discourse concerning the Unchangeable Obligations of Natural Religion; and the Truth and Certainty of the Christian Revelation* (in Watson, *A Collection of Theological Tracts* [London, 1791], vol. iv, pp. 115-123, 207-8, 213-7, 241, 243-4, 253, 285-7).

[9] *Life of George Cheyne, M. D., etc.* (Oxford, 1846), pp. 18, 30.

In this treatise, Cheyne described the elements of Newtonian philosophy in order to instruct young minds in the tenets of natural religion. The proofs of this faith were derived from the " several Parts of this admirable Fabrick of the Universe. . . ." Since man, however, was living in a state of degeneracy, the Scotch doctor held that the notions of the religion of nature required the assistance of the Christian revelation. He urged all men to imitate the life and doctrine of Jesus, which were conducive to the love of God and the practice of virtue. He also argued that universal charity was best reflected in Christianity.[10]

Besides the Latitudinarian writings of Christian rationalists, the Newtonian cosmic philosophy and the empirical psychology of Locke contributed to the greater dissemination of the deistic philosophy. The *Principia Mathematica* (1687) of Sir Isaac Newton was to the Age of Reason what the *Origin of Species* has been to our own. To the great English scientist, the universe resembled an infinite cosmic ocean containing island planets held in place by natural laws. In this cosmic sea, revolving about the sun, was a relatively small planet inhabited by man. The entire machine was created at one stroke by a brilliant Mastercraftsman who bestowed upon it a set of excellent edicts and who was able to fix and mend His Machine, if He felt it to be necessary. That God existed was a hypothesis regarded by the great Englishman as beyond doubt.[11] This cosmic philosophy emphasized just that aspect of theology which the deists made

---

[10] G. Cheyne, *Philosophical Principles, etc.* (London, 1715), pp. 89, 98-9 (Part II).

[11] Newton, *Mathematical Principles of Natural Philosophy*, tr. Motte (London, 1803), vol. ii, pp. 311-2; Burtt, *Metaphysical Foundations of Modern Science* (London, 1925), pp. 230-7, 281-95; Randall, *Making of the Modern Mind* (Boston, 1926), pp. 257-60; O. Lodge, *Pioneers of Science* (London, 1893), pp. 161-7, 180-99; and Whitehead, *Science and the Modern World* (New York, 1925), pp. 65, 68.

central.   It provided them with their concept of the Supreme
Being as an Efficient Cause of the universe.   Although they
agreed with Newton as to the existence of God, they disagreed
on His method of governing.   Whereas the English physi-
cist held that the great Mechanic could and would tinker
with His machine to perform miracles, the deists rejected
this contention on the ground that any such interference
would imply divine imperfection.   Secondly, the deistic
picture of human nature was strongly coloured by the Newtonian philosophy.   Since the English scientist had displayed
the universality of natural laws, the deists were led to feel
that religious principles were also all-pervading.   Inasmuch
as the Supreme Being acted always according to general
edicts, why should men feel that He would reveal Himself
to any particular group?   To think that God did one thing
in respect to nature and another in regard to man was considered unreasonable.   The spread of the deistic philosophy
was further stimulated by John Locke's analysis of knowledge.   Interested in acquiring certain and accurate, instead
of supposed information, the great English empiricist made
a plea for reason against reliance on blind authority in his
Essay Concerning Human Understanding (1690).   In line
with his general position, he rejected the doctrine of innate
ideas because it would " take men off the use of reason and
judgment and put them upon believing and taking upon trust
without further examination."   Even the idea that God
existed was not innate but came to the mind as the result
of reason built upon the solid foundation of experience.
Reason was to be used especially in matters pertaining to
religion in order to purge the latter of all absurdities and
superstitions.   The truths of Christianity, he held, were to
be found in its Biblical revelation which ought to be freely
investigated to ascertain whether its statements were according to, above, or contrary to reason.   Like Locke, the deists

were willing to reject everything in the Bible that was contrary to reason; but, unlike him, they were unwilling to accept anything in the Scriptures which was " mysterious " or above reason.   In short, deistic thinkers, though taking their cue from the renowned " scientist of human nature ", went beyond him by refusing to subscribe to anything in the Christian revelation which was out of harmony with their own views as to what constituted reason.

Locke's suggestion of freely investigating the Bible in order to find out if its statements were according to, above, or contrary to reason was taken up by one of his professed disciples, John Toland.   So objectionable was Toland's *Christianity Not Mysterious* (1696) that it was condemned to the flames by the Irish House of Commons and declared to be a nuisance by the Grand Jury of Middlesex.   In this book " the first important representative of the [deistic] school " [12] argued that if any miracle contained a logical contradiction it was false and consequently was not to be regarded as part of Christianity.   Anything beyond the reach of rationality was likewise not to be included, for whatever the Deity did not desire to reveal clearly was not worth knowing.   A " fictitious " miracle, like the birth of Christ, being contrary to and above reason, was to be rejected.[13] Still more outspoken in his attack upon traditional Christianity was another disciple of Locke, Anthony Collins (1676-1729), whose *Discourse of the Grounds and Reasons of the Christian Religion* (1724) called forth thirty-five answers. A " gentleman by birth, education and fortune ", Collins was a sincere freethinker who was driven to attack the religion of his birth because of his intense dislike of clerical activities.

[12] J. H. Overton and F. Relton, *English Church from the Ascession of George I to the End of the Eighteenth Century*, p. 35.

[13] J. Toland, *Christianity Not Mysterious* (London, 1696), pp. 6, 124, 150, 152.

His hostility toward the priesthood was summarized in the words of Grotius whom he quoted as saying, " Ecclesiastical history consists of nothing but the wickedness of the governing Clergy." In order to strip the priestly classes of their pretensions to authority, he proposed to examine one of the props upon which the divine origin of the Christian religion itself was based—the argument from prophecy. He held that many of the predictions which Christianity was to fulfill, specifically in regard to the Messiahship of Jesus, could not possibly be accepted. For instance, Jesus did not fulfill literally the prophecy that " out of Egypt have I call'd my son ", although Matthew told the story of Christ being carried to that land. According to Collins, the quotation referred only to the calling of the children of Israel out of Egypt.[14] The argument from miracles was then subjected to a searching analysis by Thomas Woolston (1669-1733) in his six *Discourses on the Miracles of our Saviour* (1727-9). So popular were these tracts that three successive editions of them were made, each edition consisting of ten thousand copies.[15] Because of the "levity" of his work, Woolston, a former Fellow at Cambridge, was fined and imprisoned for blasphemy. To prevent the clergy from hiding behind " the Miracles of Our Saviour ", he proposed to show that from a literal viewpoint those miracles were " full of Absurdities, Improbabilities, and Incredibilities. . . ." According to Woolston, even the Church Fathers felt that the supernatural acts of Jesus could only be taken figuratively and that if they were not so interpreted, they were both foolish and harmful.[16] Thus, just as Collins had cast doubt on a

[14] A. Collins, *Discourse of the Grounds and Reasons of the Christian Religion* (London, 1724), pp. 46-7. See also pp. 40-6, 47-8.

[15] Voltaire, *Letters on the Christian Religion* (New York, no date), p. 30.

[16] For Woolston's examination of the various miracles of Jesus consult his *A Discourse on the Miracles of Our Saviour* (London, 1727), pp. 22-30, 32-50.

literal explanation of prophecies, so had Woolston done in reference to miracles. In view of the work of these two men, clergymen approached the subject of miracles and prophecies more cautiously.[17]

While Woolston and Collins were attempting to destroy Christianity by pulling down its structure of revelation, Tindal, Chubb and Wollaston were endeavoring " to save " it by pointing out those elements in the Christian faith which could be retained as true. Matthew Tindal (1657-1733), a Fellow at Oxford, was by far the most important writer of the deistic school; in fact, his work *Christianity as Old as the Creation* (1730) was regarded as " the deist Bible ". To Tindal, both revealed and natural religion aimed to advance " the honor of God and the good of Man . . .", but the former differed from the latter in that it was not founded upon the " Nature and Reason of things, but . . . on mere will and pleasure. . . ." If any revealed faith varied from natural religion even in the minutest detail that alone was sufficient to condemn it and make support of it ineffectual. Moreover, serious questions could be raised concerning the truth of revealed religion, since there was always the possibility that it had been falsified by its disciples and changed during the centuries. In short, the deistic religion of nature was superior to the accepted supernatural evidences of Christianity. Tindal urged that all Christians should attempt to rid their religion of superstitious additions so that the true religion of Jesus—the religion of nature—might be restored.[18] Tindal's desire to return to the simple teachings of Jesus was echoed by Thomas Chubb (1679-1747) in his *True Gospel of Jesus Christ Asserted* (1738). Unlike most of the deists, who were drawn from the aristocracy or the

---

[17] McGiffert, *Protestant Thought Before Kant*, p. 219.

[18] Tindal, *Christianity as Old as the Creation* (London, 1731), pp. 52, 60, 222-3.

bourgeoisie, Chubb was an artisan and his views were naturally a reflection of his background. His position was the practical stand of a worker who saw in the Gospel a simple and hopeful creed stripped of all speculative niceties.[19] Chubb argued that the unadorned teachings of Jesus had been perverted by an emphasis upon established beliefs, rites and ceremonies as well as by the growth of an ecclesiastical organization more interested in temporal than spiritual matters. The true gospel was simple and easy to follow. It consisted of three things: (1) the practice of an eternal rule of conduct based on reason; (2) a repentance of and reformation from sin; and (3) a belief in immortality. Thus, like Tindal, Chubb, fearful that " virtue and religion were in danger of being plucked by the roots " desired to save both by returning to the simple gospel of Jesus, a gospel founded on reason and warmed by love.[20] Simplicity in religion was likewise the message of William Wollaston (1659-1724), a well-to-do schoolmaster who had taken Anglican orders. In his *Religion of Nature Delineated,* he held that all sin was ultimately the result of fallacious logic. So firmly convinced was he that correct reasoning or truth was basic to faith that he made it the essence of natural religion. This he defined as " the pursuit of happiness by the practice of reason and truth. . . ." For those who did not receive their just deserts in this world, Wollaston provided a future state where all would be compensated for their goodness. As all transgression was ultimately error, so the substance of religion was the rational worship of God.[21]

[19] Abbey and Overton, *English Church in the Eighteenth Century,* pp. 202, 204.

[20] Chubb, *True Gospel of Jesus Christ Asserted* (London, 1738), pp. 18-9, 104-5, 140-1, 155, 164-5, 167-8, 181-2.

[21] Wollaston, *Religion of Nature Delineated* (London, 1738), pp. 25, 40, 52, 126, 203.

Shaftesbury, Pope and Bolingbroke were in entire harmony with the mild tone of English deism. These men were chiefly interested in the problem of morality and only casually concerned with that of revelation. In his very popular *Characteristics of Men, Manners, Opinions, Times,* Lord Shaftesbury (1671-1713) based the distinction of right and wrong upon reason which showed men the need of doing good not because of the fear of future punishments but because of the promotion of their own happiness. Although convinced that a future state was not needed to make the good virtuous, this liberal nobleman prudently held that such a concept was necessary to compel the generality of men to live morally. Under the title of Christianity, Shaftesbury included superstition and fanaticism. Furthermore, he declared that the more he pondered upon its mysteries the more heterodox his opinions became.[22] Without realizing it, Alexander Pope in his *Essay on Man* (1733) reproduced the deistic position of Shaftesbury. The son of a Roman Catholic father, the celebrated poet was reared among Catholics who encouraged him to write. With literary success in London, he became a member of the Scriblerus Club. At about this time, his friend, Bolingbroke, who was likewise a member of the same organization, suggested to Pope that he write a philosophic poem. This he consented to do and the result was his *Essay on Man,* the arguments of which were probably furnished by Bolingbroke. In this work, Pope held that virtue made for happiness which, in turn, consisted not only in the good of one but in the felicity of all. Although he agreed that good deeds were not always rewarded in this world, he felt that virtue was too noble an object to be rewarded in temporal goods. In fact, all was right in this best of all possible worlds where everything

[22] Shaftesbury, *Characteristics, etc.,* ed. J. M. Robertson (London, 1900), vol. i, pp. 27, 66, 72, 252-3, 255, 267, 270-4; vol. ii, p. 88.

fitted into its place, all " parts of one stupendous whole, whose body nature is, and God the soul." [23]   When Pope found that this poem was generally interpreted as an apology for freethinking, he was greatly alarmed and was very grateful to Warburton when the latter defended his orthodoxy.   To the " tuneful Pope " the politically conservative Bolingbroke (1678-1751) addressed his *Essays Philosophical and Theological,* which were collected and published after his death. Voltaire's charge that the English Viscount held " the Christian religion in horror " [24] was only partly true because Bolingbroke believed the gospel of Jesus to be worthy of high praise.   To him, it was founded on the principle of universal benevolence and consequently was in accord with the laws of nature.   Yet, the simple teachings of Christ were corrupted by a "motley crowd of Jews and heathens " who added " a leaven of . . . theology."   With these views he assailed organized Christianity with its priesthood and theological subtleties. [25]

The publication of Lord Bolingbroke's essays (1752-4) marked the peak of the deistic movement in England.   Up to the middle of the eighteenth century, deism had spread widely among rich and poor, learned and unlearned.   About 1750, an orthodox German traveler, citing the *British Magazine,* stated that half of the educated people of England were deists.   Some twenty years before, a proclamation by the college heads of Oxford lamented the progress of deism among the student body. [26]   In a like fashion, deistic specula-

---

[23] Pope, *Essay on Man* (in J. A. Richards, *Outline of Knowledge* [New York, 1924], vol. xi, pp. 295, 316, 318).

[24] Voltaire, *Letters on the Christian Religion,* p. 32.

[25] Bolingbroke, *Works,* ed. Mallet (London, 1754), vol. iv, pp. 193, 267-8, 275-6, 282, 394, 629.

[26] J. M. Robertson, *A Short History of Freethought* (New York, 1906), vol. ii, pp. 136, 166.

tion had made its way among the uncultured and poorer classes, as the work of Chubb during the decade of the 'thirties indicated. Although deistic literature was read during the latter half of the eighteenth century [27] and a group of freethinkers opened a short-lived deistic chapel in London (1776), deism ceased to be a dangerous rival of orthodoxy. It was, however, still fashionable among the upper classes who seemed to have effected a cautious and tacit compromise whereby aristocratic freethinkers might be allowed to let their friends know quite openly their opinions on revelation but might not be permitted to publish any book on such a matter.[28] Thus, deistic thought merely declined in importance after 1750; it had made much too profound an impression to disappear entirely.

The decline of deism in England was due to its failure to appeal to the people and to its middle-of-the-road character. The deistic approach was so cautious, its speculation so vague that the possibility of its ever becoming a mass movement was negligible. In place of Christianity, the deists had nothing to offer. They urged the people " to follow nature ", the guide of true religion. This indefinite call scarcely impressed the public mind which desired a definitive presentation and an explicit set of rules and beliefs. Such a message was offered by Wesley's evangelical movement which gathered momentum especially after 1740. Wesley addressed himself to the hearts and not the minds of men, and his followers, unlike their deistic rivals, worked among the new industrial classes instead of rendering lip-service to the gospel of humanity. Their activities in this respect probably did a great deal to prevent skeptical thoughts from lodging them-

---

[27] Bolingbroke was widely read as late as 1790, while the translation of Voltaire's works kept alive the deistic spirit.

[28] Benn, *History of English Rationalism in the Nineteenth Century* (London, 1906), vol. i, p. 210.

selves in the minds of men, women and children. Deism found itself confronted not only by emotionalism in religion but by extreme rationalistic skepticism. Such doubters as Hume felt that the deists were too moderate in their treatment of the questions of the existence of God and the immortality of the soul. Thus, deism, caught between two uncompromising currents, was unable to defend itself successfully against the attacks of either evangelists or extreme skeptics.[29]

From England, deistic speculation made its way to France under the guidance of Voltaire. French deism, unlike the English, was so militantly anti-Christian that it paved the way for the extreme skepticism of the atheistic d'Holbach group. The aggressive deistic assault upon Christianity was chiefly due to the prevalence of an intense anti-clericalism. In eighteenth-century France, the Catholic Church held a great deal of land and her clergy were considered members of the privileged order, the First Estate. Her bishops, archbishops and abbots, drawn from the nobility, lived in ease and magnificence in direct contrast to conditions prevalent among the lowly curates. The abuses within the Church were seized upon by liberal philosophers, who, in the hope of reforming the old regime, hammered away at one of its most important props. French thinkers especially viewed with envy and alarm the political power exercised by the Jesuits whom they bitterly assailed. During the reign of Louis XV, the Society of Jesus was opposed not only by the philosophical party but also by Jansenists and Gallicans. Unlike the Jesuits, the former believed in the doctrine of conversion-by-the-will-of-God, while the latter claimed that the pope

[29] Benn, *History of English Rationalism in the Nineteenth Century*, vol. i, pp. 176-7; Abbey and Overton, *English Church in the Eighteenth Century*, pp. 236-7; and McGiffert, *Rise of Modern Religious Ideas* (New York, 1921), pp. 22-3, 41.

had no right to depose or interfere with temporal rulers and that in spiritual matters a general council of bishops was superior to the pontiff. The struggle between these two groups and the Jesuits tended to undermine ecclesiastical and civil authority as well as religious beliefs. Much to the satisfaction of Jansenists and Gallicans Louis XV eventually suppressed the Jesuit order. The king's action was also hailed by the philosophical party which saw in it a victory for enlightenment and a defeat for bigotry. During the eighteenth century, the church naturally frowned upon external divergences of opinion and was even willing to take aggressive steps to stamp these out. Yet, she was conveniently oblivious to latitudinarian views within her ranks. Inside of the Church, a goodly number of Abbé Gaimes could be found from whom eager Rousseaus could learn their deistic lessons. Again, the Gallican establishment harbored some atheistic priests, men like the Abbé Meslier, who, during the French Revolution, was described in a decree of the National Convention as " the first priest who had the courage and honesty to abjure religious errors."

The deistic speculation of Voltaire, most renowned exponent of French deism, represented essentially a cautious compromise based on common sense. During his three-year stay in England (1726-29), the French thinker came in contact with the science of Newton, the psychology of Locke and the militant deism of Collins and Woolston; all of which he brought back to and popularized in France. Although in his *Letters on the English* and in his numerous novels, Voltaire showed his deistic leanings it was not until the Calas affair that he, then almost seventy, proposed to prove the invalidity of the Christian revelation and thereby destroy the base upon which clerical authority rested. Up to this time, Voltaire was willing to compromise with the Church even to the extent of enduring her " absurd " creeds and

ceremonies. In return he asked only one thing of her and
that was the practice of tolerance. When she flouted this in
the case of Jean Calas, Voltaire decided to take the offensive.
His *Treatise on Toleration,* written during this period, was
followed up with a Niagara of pamphlets, histories, catechisms, dialogues, fables and sermons assailing the authenticity and reliability of the Bible upon which the Church
rested her claim of divine power. In these works, Voltaire
made no fine distinctions between Christianity and the
Christian Church. Never vague, he openly declared that
whereas it had taken twelve men to plant the Christian
religion, it would only take one to destroy it. Representing
the universe as a vast machine and mankind as " a very little
thing ", he repudiated miracles as contrary to natural laws.
Moreover, the supernatural acts attributed to Jesus were not
superior to those performed by the ancients. Furthermore,
Voltaire argued that the establishment of Christianity was
accompanied by the introduction of intolerance and the rejection of such " a just man " as Jesus who himself was ill-
treated " by envious doctors, and condemned to die by preju-
diced magistrates." Holding that theological beliefs were
conducive to bigotry, he vented his spleen upon them and
charged that they led to atheism by concocting " the most
absurd ideas of God." [30]

Voltaire's opposition to atheism was as intense as his hostility toward organized Christianity. To him, common
sense dictated the existence of an intelligent Being who was
responsible for the creation of the harmonious order of
nature. Beyond the view that God existed, Voltaire came to
no definite metaphysical conclusions. Always practical, he

---

[30] F. M. A. deVoltaire, *Philosophical Dictionary* (London, 1765), pp.
24-5, 87, 232-4, 280, 282, 314; *Romances,* ed. Komroff (New York, 1928),
pp. 47, 125; *Toleration and Other Essays,* tr. McCabe (New York, 1912),
p. 101; and *Letters on the Christian Religion,* p. 33.

refused " to waste his time " upon the problem of reconciling immutable natural laws with free will and contented himself with the common-sense reply that men possessed some liberty. In a like fashion, he at first satisfied himself with the consoling " tout est bien " philosophy in answer to the disconcerting question of how evil could prevail in spite of the existence of a good God.   However, the Lisbon earthquake in 1755 led him to reject this rather convenient response.   Faced by the old dilemma that God can prevent evil and will not, or He wishes to prevent it and cannot, Voltaire floundered about and ended by stripping the Deity of all His positive attributes. This led the less cautious Diderot and d'Holbach to the logical conclusion that the time had come to end the " myth " of God.   Such was the message of the latter in his *System of Nature* (1770), a book which was bitterly assailed by the thoroughly frightened Voltaire who felt that if the idea that God existed was done away with, the concept of a future state would likewise have to go.   This would mean the removal of a powerful check upon the actions of the " canaille " who chiefly did good either because they hoped to be rewarded or feared to be punished.   Thus, the prudent Voltaire concluded that if God did not exist, it would be necessary to invent Him.   To the atheists, this was common sense with a vengeance.

Voltaire was read in America especially after 1763.   His *Philosophical Dictionary, Letters on the English* and *Candide* were sold in Boston, New York and Albany.   At the same time, they were at the disposal of the members of New York and Philadelphia library societies.[31]   An interest in

[31] Voltaire's works were sold in Boston by Cox and Berry (*Catalogue,* 1776, probable date, p. 27) ; Blake (*Catalogue,* 1796, p. 41) ; and Knox (*Mass. Hist. Proceedings,* vol. lxi, p. 256) ; in New York by Rivington (*Mass. Hist. Proceedings,* vol. lxi, p. 256) ; Gaine (*Catalogue,* 1792, p. 14) ; and Berrian (*Catalogue,* 1803, p. 40) ; and in Albany by Thomas, Andrews

the treatises of the cynical Frenchman was reflected not only in library catalogues but also in newspaper advertisements and magazine articles. His writings were announced in the journals of Philadelphia, New York, Providence, New Haven and Baltimore,[32] while magazines discussed his life and conduct. Unsympathetic character studies of Voltaire appeared in numerous magazines [33] as well as anecdotes concerning his life.[34] The death of the great freethinker especially appeared to be of interest to Americans who desired to know whether he had been buried as a deist or a Christian. Newspaper and magazine articles appeared to agree that Voltaire died denying the divinity of Jesus.[35] His writings as well as his life were scrutinized and evaluated by American

and Penniman (*Catalogue*, 1798, probable date, p. 22). See also the *Library Co. Philadelphia Catalogue* 1770 and the *N. Y. Society Library Catalogue*, 1789. As early as 1771, Ezra Stiles was reading Voltaire's *Philosophical Dictionary* (E. Stiles, *Literary Diary*, ed. Dexter [New York, 1901], vol. i, p. 181).

[32] *Pennsylvania Journal and Weekly Advertiser*, July 6, 1769 (no. 1387); *The New York Journal*, December 22, 1768 (no. 1355); *The Providence Gazette, etc.*, May 7, 1785 (no. 1114); *The Connecticut Journal*, September 22, 1784 (no. 882); and the *Maryland Gazette or Baltimore Advertiser*, February 3, 1786 (no. 179).

[33] *The Pennsylvania Magazine*, January, 1775, vol. i, pp. 19-20; *The Boston Magazine*, July, 1784, vol. i, pp. 361-3; *The American Apollo*, April 20, 1792, vol. i, p. 171; *The American Universal Magazine*, August 7, 1797, vol. iii, pp. 204-6; and the *General Assembly's Missionary Magazine, etc.*, September, 1805, vol. i, pp. 455-6.

[34] *The Connecticut Journal*, Jan. 19, 1785 (no. 899); *The Moral and Sentimental Magazine*, July 3, 1797, vol. i, p. 24; and the *Literary Museum or Monthly Magazine*, Feb., 1797, p. 99.

[35] For newspaper narratives see *The Country Journal and Poughkeepsie Advertiser*, August 5, 1788 (no. 157) and the *Oriental Trumpet, etc.*, November 21, 1799. For magazine accounts refer to *The Boston Magazine*, July, 1784, vol. i, pp. 362-3; *The Columbian Magazine*, August, 1788, vol. ii, pp. 446-7; and the *General Assembly's Missionary Magazine, etc.*, January, 1806, vol. ii, pp. 30-2. Consult also, S. Payson, *Proofs of the Real Existence, etc.* (Charlestown, 1802), pp. 60-1.

critics.   While the aggressively anti-Christian Elihu Palmer
held that Voltaire was "entitled to the universal gratitude
and applause of the human race . . ." for having destroyed
"error by wholesale . . .", the more cautious John Adams
believed him to be "a little cracked." In *The American
Museum, or Repository* for July 1792, a reviewer warned
his readers not "to cultivate any close acquaintance with so
erroneous and seductive an author."

The approach of Jean Jacques Rousseau toward revelation was more in harmony with the generally mild tenor of
American deism than was that of Voltaire.   Unlike his
skeptical contemporary, the citizen of Geneva approached the
problem of religion through the conscience and not the reason
of man.   The existence of God could not be demonstrated
like a geometric proposition but was traced upon every
heart in letters that could never be effaced.   " He remains at
an equal distance from my senses and my understanding ";
wrote Rousseau, "the more I think of him, the more am I
confounded . . . I feel him. . . ."   Moreover, unlike Voltaire, Rousseau's attitude toward Christianity was one of
reverential awe.   In his *Profession of Faith of a Savoyard
Vicar*,[36] the author of *Emile* said that the greatest works of
philosophy paled into insignificance besides the Gospels.
True enough, the New Testament contained contradictions
but before these one was to remain ever "modest and cir-
cumspect: [to] regard in silence what cannot be either dis-
proved or comprehended, to humble [one's self] before the
Supreme Being, who alone knows the truth. . . ."   To
Rousseau, the essence of religion was the worship of God
and therefore creeds based on books, prophecies and miracles

[36] The Abbé Gaime was the source of Rousseau's inspiration.   From
this clergyman the good Jean Jacques learned "lessons of pure morality"
which were "as so many seeds of virtue and religion." Rousseau, *Confessions*, Hedouin Edition (London, no date), bk. i, pp. 79-81.

were of secondary importance. If Christians attempted to prove the validity of their own revelation, Jews and Mohammedans would do likewise. In the end people would not know which to follow. Thus, away with " artificial faith ", let men follow the correct path of natural religion.[37] On the whole, Rousseau's skepticism was superior to the biting mockery of Voltaire which only irritated all who were seriously religious. Yet, Rousseau's emotional approach gave the orthodox a weapon which they could equally brandish over the heads of atheists and deists. To the atheistic denial of God as well as to the deistic rejection of the Christian revelation the faithful could easily reply, " We believe! "

The prudent skepticism of Rousseau was more acceptable to American deists than the militant freethinking of Voltaire. In 1765, John Adams referred to Rousseau as an " opponent of feudalism "; by 1771 and 1772, the *Emile* was sold in South Carolina, Virginia, Pennsylvania and New York.[38] Anecdotes in praise of the " sublime Author of the Emilius " appeared in Philadelphia and Baltimore periodicals, while his literary qualities were likewise reviewed in the magazines of the period.[39] *The Amercan Museum, or Repository* for July 1792, however, contained an article which suggested that, while Rousseau should be read, he was not to be taken too seriously because he was an enemy of revelation. *The Connecticut Evangelical Magazine* for

[37] Rousseau, *Emilius and Sophia* (London, 1783), vol. ii, pp. 267-8; vol. iii, p. 49; *Profession of Faith of a Savoyard Vicar* (New York, 1889), pp. 34-5, 38, 56, 61, 64, 74-5, 76.

[38] B. Faÿ, *Revolutionary Spirit in France and America* (New York, 1928), p. 40 and L. Rosenthal, *Rousseau in Philadelphia* (*Magazine of American History*, vol. xii, pp. 51-2).

[39] *The Boston Magazine*, April, 1784, vol. i, p. 220; *The American Universal Magazine*, May 15, 1797, vol. ii, p. 224; and the *Baltimore Weekly Magazine*, July 19, 1800, p. 97.

August 1800 was willing to admit that the Frenchman had praised Jesus very highly but felt that if he had remained an unbeliever to the end, " the pangs of an accusing conscience [would] form a state of future misery equal to the highest descriptions of the Christian scriptures." Naturally American deists used Rousseau to further their cause and consequently they reprinted his *Profession of Faith of a Savoyard Vicar.*[40]

Comte de Volney (1757-1820) was more outspoken in his rejection of Christianity than was Rousseau. A member of the Estates-General and Constituent Assembly, he achieved a reputation as a savant through the appearance of his *Ruins: or a Survey of the Revolutions of Empires* (1791). Like Voltaire, he was moved by so bitter an anti-clerical feeling that he rejected the Christian revelation and predicted the final union of all religions by the recognition of the common truth underlying them. In 1795, he came to America where he remained for two years. Here he was immediately assailed by the Unitarian Priestley then living in Philadelphia. So well was Volney's work received in America that along with Paine's *Age of Reason* it was said " to unchristianize " thousands. As a significant contribution to the rise of a more militant deistic movement in the new Republic, it will be more fully discussed in its proper place.[41] Two years after the publication of the *Ruins,* the atheistic Hébertists were praying before the altar of the Goddess of Reason, a ceremony which shocked Robespierre into proclaiming the Worship of the Supreme Being.[42] This

[40] *Prospect, or View of the Moral World* from May 5, 1804 (no. 22) to November 17, 1804 (no. 50).

[41] See chapter v, pp. 126-7.

[42] Robespierre's speech on the Supreme Being delivered on June 8, 1794 was reported in American newspapers. See chapter v, pp. 146-7.

struggle between the atheistic Hébert and the deistic Robespierre was symbolic of the battle deism had to fight in the
intellectual circles of pre-Revolutionary France where its
" real " enemy was the atheism of the d'Holbach group.

CHAPTER III

RISE OF DEISM IN COLONIAL AMERICA (1713-1763)

BESIDES the importation of European rationalistic works, the introduction of Newtonian science paved the way for the rise of deistic speculation in colonial America. The representation of the universe as a vast machine set in motion by an Efficient Cause and run according to immutable natural laws was reflected in the literature of the provincial period. In Calvinistic circles, the conservative Cotton Mather was amazed and charmed by the thought of an infinite universe with countless globes kept in place by the law of universal gravity, while Jonathan Dickinson, President of the College of New Jersey, praised "the glorious art and contrivance of [this] admirable frame of nature. . . ." The liberal-minded Mayhew, a Boston preacher, wrote likewise of the regularity, beauty and harmony of the natural. A young deist, Franklin, noted the insignificance of "this little ball on which we move. . . ." Some twenty-eight years later, John Adams, who in his youth showed deistic inclinations, wrote that the "solar system [was] but one very small wheel in the great, the astonishing machine of the world. . . ." In a like fashion, the influence of the Newtonian cosmography showed itself in Anglican surroundings. Samuel Johnson, President of King's College, saw a world system of fixed stars and our own sun "with his noble and splendid Chorus of Planets, Satellites and Comets. . . ." To William Smith, described by Ezra Stiles as "a consummate Hypocrite in Religion and Politics", it appeared ridiculous to watch "the atom-lords of this atom world . . . strut about in pride. . . ." [1]

---

[1] C. Mather, *Christian Philosopher* (London, 1721), pp. 16, 18, 21, 81-2;

The *Principia Mathematica* and popular tracts explaining it occupied a prominent place on the shelves of colonial libraries.[2]   One provincial scholar, Cadwallader Colden, even proceeded to criticize and enlarge upon it.   American students were advised by Mather and Johnson to read Newton, "our perpetual dictator. . . ."   Clap, Rector of Yale, described the celebrated Englishman as a "great Genius", while the poetic Livingston, who was later to become Governor of New Jersey, sang of the "Immortal Newton; whose illustrious name will shine on records of eternal fame."[3] Since the Newtonian system was based on the Copernican theory, the latter was generally accepted; in 1714, Mather was preaching it from his Boston pulpit much to the distress of Samuel Sewall who thought that it was distinctly out of place.   The Copernican theory was popularized in colonial almanacs, while the writings of its chief exponents, Brahe, Kepler, Galileo, Descartes, Boyle and Whiston were either to be found in provincial libraries or referred to in the litera-

J. Dickinson, *Reasonableness of Christianity* (Boston, 1732), pp. 17-9, 25, 27-8; J. Mayhew, *Two Sermons, etc.* (Boston, 1763), pp. 27, 41; B. Franklin, *Works*, ed. Sparks (Boston, 1836), vol. ii, pp. 1-2; J. Adams, *Works*, ed. C. F. Adams (Boston, 1850), vol. ii, p. 15; S. Johnson, *Introduction to the Study of Philosophy* (New London, 1743), p. 18; and W. Smith, *Discourses* (London, 1762), pp. 84-6 (Appendix).

[2] *Yale Catalogue*, 1714 (in Wright, *Literary Culture in Early New England*, p. 185) and 1743 (in Clap, a *Catalogue of Yale College*, p. 10); *Johnson Catalogue* (MS.), 1726; *Byrd Catalogue* (in Bassett, *Writings of William Byrd, etc.*, p. 441) and the *Library Co. of Philadelphia Catalogue*, 1764, p. 51. For works used to explain Newton see Byrd (in Basset, *op. cit.*, p. 436) and the *Library Co. of Philadelphia Catalogue*, 1764, pp. 33, 93.

[3] T. Clap, *Essay on the Nature and Foundation of Moral Virtue* (New Haven, 1765), p. 46; S. Johnson, *Introduction to the Study of Philosophy*, p. 28; W. Livingston, *Philosophic Solitude* (New York, 1747), p. 39; and C. Mather, *Student and Preacher, etc.* (London, 1789), p. 125. See also the *American Magazine*, January, 1745, for an account of Newton's life, pp. 9-18.

ture of the period.[4] As in England and France, so in
America, the Newtonian cosmic philosophy furnished the
deists with their central concept of God as a Passive Police-
man. From this view, it was intellectually very easy to rule
out miracles altogether, a position which was adopted by the
champions of the new dispensation and which marked a significant deviation from the teachings of their professed
Master. In still another way, American deists used the work
of the English scientist to advance their own views. Newton had demonstrated that the Supreme Being always acted
according to general edicts. Then why, asked the deists,
should men feel that He should reveal Himself to any particular group and therefore do one thing in respect to Nature
and another thing in regard to man? The advent of colonial
deism was further made possible by the empirical psychology
of Locke. Like Newton's *Principia Mathematica,* Locke's
Essay Concerning Human Understanding had a great vogue
in provincial America. It was listed in library catalogues
and frequently alluded to in literary works.[5] By making

[4] N. Ames, *Astronomical Diary,* 1733 (Boston, 1733) ; J. Taylor,
Pennsilvania, 1743 (Philadelphia, 1743) ; *Harvard Catalogue,* 1723 (in
Wright, *op. cit.,* pp. 272, 279, 289) ; *Yale Catalogue,* 1743 (in Clap,
op. cit., pp. 8, 10) ; Byrd, *Catalogue* (in Bassett, *op. cit.,* pp. 436, 441) ;
Lee Library, 1694; *Sharpe Catalogue,* 1713 (in N. Y. Hist. Collections
for 1880 (New York, 1881), p. 362; *Library Co. of Philadelphia Catalogue,*
1764, p. 57; *Johnson Catalogue* (MS.), 1726; Mather, *Student and
Preacher,* pp. 125, 128; *Christian Philosopher,* pp. 20, 44, 227; S. Johnson,
Introduction, etc., p. 29; and W. Nadir, *Mercurius Novanglicanus,* 1743
(Boston, 1743).

[5] *Yale Catalogue,* 1714 (in Wright, *op. cit.,* p. 185) and 1743 (in Clap,
op. cit., p. 5) ; and *Johnson Catalogue,* 1726 (MS.). Both Franklin and
Adams possessed copies of the work. (B. Franklin, *Writings,* ed. Smyth,
vol. x, p. 149 and J. Adams, *Works,* ed. C. F. Adams, vol. ii, p. 88).
References were made to the essay by T. Clap, *Essay on the Nature, etc.,*
p. 25; J. Edwards, *Works,* ed. S. L. Dwight, vol. ii, p. 207; J. Dickinson,
Reasonableness of Christianity, p. 15; C. Chauncy, *Benevolence of the
Deity* (Boston, 1784), pp. 92, 97-100; and S. Johnson, *Introduction, etc.,*
pp. 8, 27.

reason the final standard of appeal, Locke supplied American deists with a weapon which could be used to destroy the validity of the Biblical evidences.

With the introduction of the new science and psychology as well as with the importation of English rationalistic works, a critical attitude emerged in Calvinistic and Anglican circles. In the former, an attack was made upon Puritan theology which ended in the rise of a deistic literature implicitly anti-Christian. From 1691 to 1763, the Puritan tradition in Massachusetts was considerably weakened. The participation of the ministry in the unfortunate Salem tragedy of 1692 tended to lessen clerical influence. It furnished liberals with an ever-handy citation designed to illustrate the dangers of ecclesiastical bigotry and superstition. At the opening of the eighteenth century, Cotton Mather, who played a prominent role in the Salem affair, feeling the power slipping from "the hands of godly men", attempted to protect the theocratic heritage of the Bay colony by advocating a closer union of the churches. In 1705, he proposed the formation of ministerial associations which were to give pastors advice, license clerical candidates and examine all charges against clergymen. Furthermore, Mather suggested that lay and ministerial delegates to these associations were to constitute standing councils to consider all matters arising within their limits. All decisions of these councils were to be final. These proposals, however, encountered opposition not only in Massachusetts but also in England where the Puritan commonwealths were especially unpopular. When it was suggested that a synod be called to determine church policies, the home government refused to consent. Imperial intervention not only dashed the hopes of the Mathers but also secured concessions for those dissenting from the Congregational order. By an act of 1727, Anglicans were allowed limited exemption in the Bay Colony. Although ministerial rates were to be collected as usual, the money of those who lived within five miles of an Anglican Church was to be turned over by the collectors to Anglican ministers. In 1728 and 1729, Quakers were likewise exempted provided they attended Church on Sunday, lived within five miles of a place of worship and declared their faith in the divine inspiration of the Bible and the Trinitarian doctrine.[6]

In Connecticut, the old order was more firmly entrenched. With the Church and State working together, a plan of " Consociation " similar to that of the Mathers was adopted. In 1708, the Saybrook Synod drew up a scheme which provided for the organization of the Congregational Churches through associations and consociations. The former were composed of pastors and elders in a rather extended territory, while the latter were unions of churches within more limited areas. In the same year, a Toleration Act was passed which cautiously declared that nothing in the act was to be interpreted to the prejudice of the established church or to the exclusion of any person from paying any ministerial or town dues, as might thereafter be requested. This Toleration Act was of little benefit to the Baptists, Quakers or Anglicans who as they increased in numbers demanded and worked for a greater degree of freedom. In 1727, Anglican churchmen were exempted from the payment of taxes used in the building of churches. Two years later, exemption was granted to the Baptists and Quakers. This, however, did not mean toleration for dissenters; in 1742, the Act of 1708 was temporarily repealed, only to be put in force again in 1760.[7]

[6] S. M. Reed, *Church and State in Massachusetts, 1691-1740* (University of Illinois Studies in the Social Sciences, vol. iii, no. 4, Dec., 1914), pp. 132, 135, 139, 180, 185, 189; and W. Walker, *History of the Congregational Churches in the United States* (New York, 1884), pp. 202-4.

[7] M. L. Greene, *Rise of Religious Liberty in Connecticut* (Boston, 1905), pp. 138-43, 147, 154.

The outstanding event in the religious history of provincial New England was the Great Awakening. It began in 1734 with the preaching of Jonathan Edwards in the town of Northampton, Massachusetts. A few years later, this work was reenforced by the great Methodist preacher, George Whitefield. Both men attempted to draw individuals from the surface aspects of traditional dogma and formal observance to a deeper spiritual experience. The Great Awakening brought out two important tendencies in religious thought, both of which worked against the old Puritan system. One group, swept away by the emotional appeal of the evangelists, broke away from the established churches. The " New Lights " were bitterly assailed by a group of rationalists who drew their strength from the sophisticated society of the older towns. Some of these men, like Wigglesworth, were firm believers in the old ecclesiastical order, while others, like Chauncy, reacted strongly against some of the main tenets of orthodox Calvinism. Yet, both conservatives and liberals vigorously assailed "enthusiasm". In his *Seasonable Thoughts on the State of Religion in New England* (1743), Charles Chauncy, a Boston clergyman, called upon his clerical associates to eradicate such " dangerous " tendencies as itinerant preaching, "uncomfortable . . . Animosities " and physical agitations or " extraordinaries ". In order to check the revivalistic trend, he proposed that the " New Lights " be excluded from the pulpits of organized churches, that ministerial candidates be examined, and that certain basic doctrines be accepted after a rational investigation. He bitterly denounced the work of Whitefield as " a Dishonour to true Religion. . . ." Wigglesworth likewise condemned evangelicalism by asserting that it was subversive of Christianity, since every man imagined that any thought, which he strongly felt, came from God, although he had no proof of it.[8]

[8] Chauncy, *Seasonable Thoughts on the State of Religion in New*

The rationalistic movement was, for the most part, liberal in tendency; it criticized the principal tenets of the orthodox Puritan creed—original sin, predestination and, finally, the doctrine of the Trinity. It sought to humanize faith by representing the Deity as a benevolent Being and man as a responsible agent. According to contemporary accounts, its anti-Calvinistic or so-called " Arminian " teachings circulated in Cambridge, Northampton and other prominent Massachusetts towns. In the case of Cambridge, these reports seem to be somewhat exaggerated; at least, up to the Revolution Harvard was far from being liberal. An able scholar, Christie, has shown that, during the early eighteenth century, the fears of the Mather family concerning the progress of " Arminianism" at Harvard were groundless. In 1724, Cotton Mather felt that students at the Cambridge seat of learning were reading books fit for " Satan's library ". Yet, these works were indeed harmless; they were satanic only in so far as they were secular. About two years later, the same clergyman was unable to detect a single Congregational minister who entertained " Arminian " views. The college authorities at Harvard attempted to preserve the orthodoxy of their pupils. The overseers asserted the right to examine the theological views of the instructional staff and it was indeed an innovation for them to approve the appointment of John Winthrop without examination. Wigglesworth, the first professor to occupy the Hollis chair of divinity, was questioned by Leverett and Colman. The latter was no latitudinarian in theology; in fact, in 1732, he begged a New London clergyman to vindicate Yale from the aspersion of " Arminianism." Moreover, during the provincial period, the " pious youths " of the college were taught theology by such men as

England (Boston, 1743), pp. 36-40, 55, 78, 334, 336, 340-1, 397, 414-5, 422-4; and Wigglesworth, *A Letter to the Reverend Mr. George Whitefield, etc.* (Boston, 1745), pp. 3-4, 6.

Wigglesworth, Flynt and Holyoke, all of whom were " free from liberalism." Although the latitudinarian works of Tillotson and Clarke were to be found in the Harvard library, students did not take them out. Tillotson was not drawn out for nine years (1732-1741) and Clarke for two (1739-1741). Even though Locke was used as a textbook, all the other basic texts were orthodox.[9] Furthermore, Christie has shown that up to the middle of the eighteenth century there were few, if any, " Arminian " ministers in the Congregational Churches of New England. The moment anyone was suspected of " Arminianism," life was made so uncomfortable that, as in the case of Benjamin Kent of Marlborough, resignation from the pulpit resulted. Again, with the exception of Experience Mayhew's *Grace Defended* (1744), no " Arminian " book was published in America prior to 1749.[10]

Yet, from the middle of the eighteenth century onward, liberal doctrines became more current; they were preached by Gay, Briant and Mayhew at Hingham, Braintree and Boston. Ebenezer Gay, pastor at Hingham, was one outstanding New Englander who held opinions clearly outside of and distinct from Calvinism. In full sympathy with the rationalistic spirit of his age, he desired free inquiry and was opposed to all creeds. In 1759, Gay, a Dudleian lecturer at Harvard, addressed the undergraduate body on *Natural Religion as Distinguish'd from Revealed*. He defined the former as anything which reason alone discovered and the latter as anything which God had made known to man through immediate inspiration or prophetic teachings. The religion of nature consisted in adoring God and in helping His creatures. It was, however, in need of the Christian

[9] F. A. Christie, *The Beginnings of Arminianism in New England* (Papers of the American Society of Church History, 2nd ser., vol. iii, pp. 154-9).

[10] *Ibid.*, vol. iii, pp. 160-2, 165.

revelation because the reason of the average man was not equal to the task of discovering it. Yet, if the evidences of Christianity were inconsistent with " the possibility of things ", they were to be discarded.[11] Lemuel Briant, pastor of the First Church in Braintree, also reacted against the traditional Calvinism of his day and repudiated the accepted doctrine of predestination. He regarded " the pure and perfect Religion of Jesus " as built upon the assumption that man was a responsible agent whose happiness depended upon his personal actions. To disparage moral goodness was to promote " infidelity ", to encourage vice and to remove divine comfort. The very aim of God was to advance the happiness of man. Although Briant realized that his position was conducive neither to " popular Applause nor priestly Favours ", he felt that if his stand was true, it would endure forever.[12]

The reaction against traditional Puritanism was revealed not only in the writings of Briant and Gay but also in those of Mayhew and Chauncy. Influenced by Clarke and the milder English deists, Jonathan Mayhew, who, according to John Adams, " was a smart man, but embraced some doctrines not generally approv'd ", sought to advance the cause of tolerance and rationalism. To the Boston clergyman, the Deity ruled according to the standards of benevolence and wisdom. The Creator was to be obeyed not through fear but through love. His belief in divine goodness caused him to reject the idea that a majority of mankind was condemned to everlasting torments. Moreover, Mayhew held that man was responsible for all his moral actions and was answerable

---

[11] E. Gay, *Natural Religion, As Distinguish'd from Revealed* (Boston, 1759), pp. 6-7, 21-2, 29-30 and Cooke, *Unitarianism in America* (Boston, 1902), pp. 58-60.

[12] Briant, *Absurdity and Blasphemy of Depretiating Moral Virtue* (Boston, 1749), pp. 7-8, 27-8, 30-1.

to God alone. He entertained the highest regard for the teachings of Christianity whose good ends were " clearly discernible. . . ." [13] Charles Chauncy carried on the work of Mayhew. He was well versed in the deistic speculation of England and clearly reflected the rationalistic, humanitarian and freedom-loving spirit of the new liberalism. Convinced that the Deity was the epitome of love, he rejected the doctrine of the eternal damnation of sinners as contrary to the divine scheme. Man had the capacity to do good, and thus, to attain happiness. These doctrines sounded strange, to say the least, in a Calvinistic pulpit and, for a time, Chauncy hesitated to declare them openly. When he did so, he was bitterly assailed. Some of the faithful described him as a deist, while others, like Stiles of Yale, though rejecting this description, quite willingly granted that this " Learned Character " possessed " some Singularities in Theology. . . ." [14]

While these New Englanders were rejecting Puritan beliefs but accepting the Christian revelation, others—Franklin, Hawley, Adams and Bliss—were reacting against Calvinistic doctrines to such an extent as to embrace the still more " dangerous teachings " of deism. Yet, of this small band, only one, Franklin, continued throughout his life to subscribe to ideas which were more or less deistic. Even before his departure from Boston (1723), Franklin was a deist " vowed to the cult of Reason and Liberty." Having

[13] Mayhew, *Two Sermons on the Nature, Extent and Perfection of Divine Goodness*, pp. 12, 14, 24, 35-9, 61, 65-6, 78; J. Adams, *Works*, ed. C. F. Adams, vol. ii, pp. 4, 10; and Schneider, *Puritan Mind* (New York, 1930), pp. 192-7.

[14] Chauncy, *Benevolence of the Deity*, pp. 18, 39, 51, 122-6, 141, 154 *et seq.*, 244; Ezra Stiles, *Literary Diary*, ed. Dexter (New York, 1901), vol. iii, pp. 255, 326; and Schneider, *op. cit.*, pp. 198-201. For a contemporary appraisal of his life and character see *The American Museum; or Repository*, February, 1790, vol. vii, pp. 76-7.

poisoned himself with an extra-large dose of Collins and Shaftsbury, young Benjamin regarded theology as a mortal enemy and religion as a useful ally (provided it was not employed to support tyranny and superstition). He imparted his deistic views to a fellow apprentice who fell deeply in love with them. At the age of seventeen, Franklin left Boston for Philadelphia where he met William Keith, Governor of Pennsylvania, an audacious freethinker whose deism (as well as democratic politics) " shocked " the " substantial " Quaker element of the colony. Upon the advice of Keith, the young man went to London where he found employment as a printer. In the printing shop, Franklin had an excellent opportunity to view the latest books on the deistic controversy which was then reaching the peak of its popularity. One day, while setting up Wollaston's *Dissertation on Natural Religion,* he ran across the phrase " The base of all religion is the difference between the acts of men, be they good, bad or indifferent." The clever Benjamin could hardly restrain himself ; eagerly he wrote an answer to this sentence, a reply, which though not original, disclosed a penetrating mind. His *Dissertation on Liberty and Necessity, Pleasure and Pain* was a pretty little treatise composed in the geometric fashion of the day. In one hundred axioms, he proved to his own satisfaction that sin, liberty and personal immortality did not exist. An " all-wise, all-good and all-powerful God " would naturally allow only virtue to prevail and so the entire question of evil was a foolish one. Moreover, every one acted necessarily in accordance with the edicts of the deity and therefore if a thief stole something, God had to find the robber as virtuous as his victim. Yet, honest Benjamin made haste to remark " I would not be understood by this to encourage or defend theft; 'tis only for the sake of the Argument and will certainly have no *ill effect. . . .*" Since there was no difference between virtue and vice, the favorite deistic argument in support of immortality—that a future state existed so that the Supreme Being might make amends for injustices suffered by the good in this life—was rejected. Moreover the soul ceased to exist after death.[15] Benjamin carefully printed one hundred copies of this work. Later in his life he did all he could to suppress this " clever . . . performance " of his youth.

Even in London, Franklin continued his practice of going to church, a habit which persisted throughout his life. He liked to attend church meetings, for here he met people and exchanged ideas. Moreover these services, according to one of his latest biographers,[16] helped him " to maintain his prestige as a serious man " and, we might add, his reputation as a Christian. Like most American deists, Franklin was prudence personified. As a prototype of his own Poor Richard, he was too sensible to jeopardize his political and social influence by espousing views which an important group in the community abhorred. In a letter to his daughter Sarah, dated 1764, he stated that his political enemies were many. He urged his daughter to continue her attendance at church, since if she failed to do so, her indiscretions would be "magnified into crimes in order the more sensibly to wound and afflict me. . . ." With these practical considerations in mind, Franklin was likely to say very little about deism. His reserve in dealing with this topic was due not only to his desire to advance in the world but also to his growing indifference to metaphysical disputation which he came to regard as arguing for argument's sake. Doing good was far more important than proving a contention by theological or abstract subtleties.

[15] B. Franklin, *Dissertation on Liberty and Necessity, Pleasure and Pain* (in Riley, *American Philosophy—Early Schools* [New York, 1907], pp. 272-9).

[16] B. Faÿ, *Franklin* (Boston, 1929), p. 97.

Yet, in spite of his reticence in respect to deism, Franklin said enough, chiefly in confidential letters, to warrant his classification as a deist along the general lines of Lord Herbert of Cherbury. Like that seventeenth-century Englishman, Franklin was persuaded that reason was to be used to ascertain the basic principles of sound religion. These fundamental truths consisted of a belief in the existence of God, of the practice of virtue and of the immortality of the soul. He held that in all ages mankind had accepted the existence of a good and wise Deity who created men so that they might secure happiness. Felicity was to be achieved through the good life which was more important to the success of religion than was orthodoxy. Convinced that the Supreme Being was concerned in the earthly happiness of men, the American statesman was also persuaded that God was interested in their future good fortune. His belief in immortality grew stronger as he drew nearer the grave. Franklin also agreed with Lord Herbert in regard to the Christian revelation. Although he did not desire to see Christian influence diminished, Franklin thought that his creed did not require the support of supernatural evidences. Furthermore, he argued that the Christian churches had been so perverted that " outward Appearances and Professions " were held in higher esteem than the simple teachings of Jesus.[17] ·Franklin's deism was a reaction against the stern Puritan environment in which he grew up. He especially repudiated the doctrine of Calvinistic determinism on the ground that it was inconsistent with the goodness and wisdom of God. Furthermore, he was cynical of the strict-

[17] B. Franklin, *Works*, ed. J. Sparks, vol. ii, pp. 3-4, 6, 526; *Writings*, ed. Smyth, vol. i, p. 296, vol. ii, p. 215, vol. iii, p. 145, vol. iv, p. 248, vol. ix, pp. 267, 333-4, vol. x, pp. 84-5; B. Franklin, *Memoirs* (New York, 1839), vol. ii, pp. 14-6; and Curtis, *Outline of Philosophy in America* (reprinted from the Western Reserve University *Bulletin*, March, 1896, p. 5).

ness with which New England kept Sunday. This exact observance he contrasted with the freedom prevalent in Flanders where he

looked around for God's judgments, but saw no signs of them. The cities were well built . . . the markets filled with plenty, the people well favored and well clothed . . . which makes one suspect that the Deity is not so angry at that offence [non-attendance at church] as a New England Justice.[18]

In the meantime, four other New Englanders, Hawley, Adams, Bliss and Gridley were venturing along the road of skepticism. Joseph Hawley (1723-1788), a cousin of the famous Jonathan Edwards and a member of his church, went to Cambridge in 1744 and while there probably studied theology. Here, he came in contact with " a most dangerous and Corrupt Book " entitled *Grace Defended in a Modest Plea for an Important Truth*. This work was written by Experience Mayhew who held that, while salvation was only possible through the grace of God, man should be active in receiving and improving the grace that was offered. According to his own testimony, given many years later, young Hawley imbibed such " wicked principles " at Cambridge that he refused to accept " any Doctrine upon the mere authority of God's word. . . ." He showed a pronounced deistic trend in that he was unwilling to accept supernatural revelation unless it was consistent with the " Divine Light of Natural reason. . . ." By 1754, however, the embryonic deist began to retract, though it was not until 1762 that the Northampton lawyer, after an attack of religious melancholy, discarded the deistic infatuation of his youth. Hawley's change of heart was partly due to the untiring efforts of the Reverend John Hooker.[19]

[18] B. Franklin, *Writings*, ed. Smyth, vol. iv, pp. 185-6.

[19] J. Hawley, *Confession of his Belief in Arminianism* (MS.);

John Adams likewise indulged in skeptical utterances at this time. In the characteristic fashion of deistic speculation, the future President subscribed to a belief in the existence of God and in a future state. Like Bolingbroke, whom he greatly admired, the young Braintree philosopher believed that Christianity had been corrupted by synods, confessions and subscriptions. To him, the Christian churches were not producing good citizens; they were rather concentrating upon the manufacture of adepts in the solution of riddles. Although convinced that God governed the world according to universal laws, he conceded the possibility of Christian miracles.[20] Throughout his life, Adams was essentially a critical thinker who would disagree just as easily with the outstanding liberal philosophers of his age as he would with the Calvinistic clergymen of New England. He was a scholar and student who was extremely cautious in making any generalization. Like Adams, the Reverend William Bliss (1728-1808) became a skeptic during his youth. Ezra Stiles, who had quite a penchant for detecting deists, discovered that Bliss was " connected with deistical acquaintances, read deistical authors, and was deeply plunged in their system for many years. . . ." By 1765, however, the good clergyman repented of his evil ways and thereafter became a firm believer in revelation and an " earnest Advocate of Religion. . . ."[21]

Ezra Stiles was well equipped for the task of detecting the intellectual vagrancies of Christian clergymen. Like Bliss, the future president of Yale traversed as a young man the road leading from faith to doubt; yet in the end he too

Trumbull, *History of Northampton, Massachusetts* (Northampton, 1902), vol. ii, pp. 230, 543, 548; and Brown, *Joseph Hawley* (New York, 1931), pp. 19-21, 36, 41.

[20] J. Adams, *Works*, ed. C. F. Adams, vol. ii, pp. 5-8, 12, 17-8, 20.

[21] Stiles, *Literary Diary*, ed. Dexter, vol. i, p. 566.

regained the path of Christian belief. In 1750, the youthful Stiles exchanged views with another young man who raised a number of skeptical questions as to the truth of the Biblical revelation. These observations caused Stiles to feel that the Scriptures were " a fable and delusion ". Yet, these doubts did not deter him from becoming a clergyman. In the ministry, however, Stiles was unable to find peace and therefore he determined to study law. In 1753, he took the oath of an attorney but his theological interests were so intense that he continued to study the Bible. Some three years later, his doubts were resolved and thereafter he became a steadfast believer in the truth of the Christian revelation.[22] Another New Englander was likewise so beguiled by the deistic philosophy that he too drifted from the pulpit to the bar. Jeremy Gridley, well-known for his defense of the Writs of Assistance against Otis and a prominent figure in the American Masonic movement, was assailed by his contemporaries not only for his support of British policies against colonial pretensions but also for his deistic tendencies. Charles Chauncy felt that Gridley had no religion at all, while Ezra Stiles described him as " a disciple of Shaftesbury and Bolingbroke. . . ." From 1743 to 1746 Gridley published *The American Magazine and Historical Chronicle; for all the British Plantations* and " with the gracious attitude of one deist to another " presented some of Voltaire's non-controversial works.[23] Occasionally he allowed anonymous authors to use his magazine to spread deistic ideas. In one issue an unknown writer completely ignored the Christian revelation and urged his readers to follow nature which always led to God and happiness. Believing that the Deity intended to make men happy, he held that felicity could

[22] A. Holmes, *The Life of Ezra Stiles* (Boston, 1798), pp. 35-6.
[23] Richardson, *History of Early American Magazines* (New York, 1931), pp. 44, 48.

be achieved here and hereafter if people lived virtuously. Like Pope, the author argued that if any one contemplated the universe, he must be convinced that everything was excellently arranged. Moreover, he agreed with the English deist that the prevalence of folly and vice were actually beneficial because these evils gave force to moral laws among " grosser minds." [24]   A few months later, in the same periodical, another anonymous author, " Eusebius ", wrote an article entitled " The Unreasonableness of Persecution " in which he indirectly assailed Christianity. Maintaining that true religion promoted brotherly love, he argued that the Christian religion had encouraged strife and had " prov'd as brutal, bloody and inhuman as Mohametanism. . . ." " Eusebius " held that unless a tolerant attitude was adopted toward all religious beliefs, men would be driven into the ranks of " infidelity." [25]

That the seeds of deism were being sown in New England soil was the opinion of contemporary observers. In 1755, John Adams noted that the "principles of deism" were making progress in the country town of Worcester where *The Moral Philosopher,* a work written by the English deist Morgan, was circulating widely.[26]   During the course of an evening's conversation, Adams heard a speaker lightly dismiss many of the miracles of Jesus as mere stories indulged in by "enthusiasts ". Moreover, Mayhew in one of his sermons

---

[24] *The American Magazine,* December, 1744, pp. 678-80.

[25] *Ibid.,* June, 1745, pp. 255-7.

[26] Adams, *Works,* ed. C. F. Adams, vol. ii, p. 3 (note). In *The Moral Philosopher* (1737), Thomas Morgan asserted that Christianity, as first preached by Jesus, was in reality deism. He held that the simple teachings of Christ had been corrupted by his followers who had altered the gospels and had ascribed miracles to his doctrines. He rejected not only the supernatural acts of Jesus but also the idea that Christ had fulfilled the Hebraic prophecies. (T. Morgan, *The Moral Philosopher,* vol. i, pp. 350, 412, 440; vol. ii, pp. 220, 222, 225.)

felt it necessary to omit certain Biblical proofs because some of his audience were unwilling to accept the authenticity of the Christian revelation.[27] In 1759, Ezra Stiles reported that the "vitiated morals of Deism" were spreading. In order to stem the rising tide of "infidelity", he urged men to defend Christianity on the basis of its rationality. He attributed the progress of freethinking to the French and Indian War which, he claimed, had brought Americans into contact with British officers of deistic inclinations. Stiles exaggerated the skeptical proclivities of the British military leadership in America as well as its influence upon the growth of the deistic movement. British officers, like James Wolfe, when moved by a desire to do any extensive reading, turned to books dealing with military history rather than to those concerned with deism. Even though some of the English commanders were intimately acquainted with the leading freethinkers of the day, their skepticism is not established by this fact. James Abercrombie, commander of the Anglo-American forces in 1758, knew and corresponded with David Hume, yet the latter did not write to his military friend on such serious subjects as God and immortality. On the contrary, Hume satisfied himself with witty observations, personal references and plans for practical jokes.[28]

In the meantime, the New England defenders of the faith sought to check the progress of deism by pamphlets and articles in newspapers and magazines. Thomas Clap, who was so "strenuous for Orthodoxy" that "he would have supported it with the Inquisition & Arms" had he been "a Cardinal or Pontiff", defended the Christian revelation in his *Essay on the Nature and Foundations of Moral Virtue*

[27] Adams, *Works*, ed. C. F. Adams, vol. ii, p. 13 and J. Mayhew, *Two Sermons, etc.*, p. 14.

[28] Burton, *Life and Correspondence of David Hume* (Edinburgh, 1846), vol. i, pp. 212, 222, 312.

and Obligations. In this work, the Yale Rector claimed that
without the divine evidences of Christianity men would never
have known the attributes of the Deity, the true basis of
moral duties and the road to salvation.[29] A Boston periodical, *The American Magazine* for August 1744, urged the
study of the New Testament in order to combat skepticism
and supply young divinity students with correct ideas concerning the essential tenets of the Christian religion. One
year later, this same magazine carried an article entitled,
" Some Thoughts on Infidelity ", a reprint from the works
of " a late Author." The writer urged that deistic principles
be kept from the " Rabble ", who, for the most part, remained
orderly chiefly through the force of religious teachings.
He therefore requested all reasonable men to hold in con-
tempt " infidels " who became the " Idols of the Mob. . . ."
This article is illustrative of the cautious position of eighteenth-century liberals in respect to deism. So long as deistic
principles were spread among " the sober and respectable "
elements of the community, all was well. " Enlightened "
members of the aristocracy and the bourgeoisie might play
with them but not the masses, for in the hands of the latter
they might be used for revolutionary purposes. Consequently, any intellectual who popularized deism stamped
himself, so far as the upper classes were concerned, as an
enemy of society. In the same Boston magazine, a few
months later, a correspondent, " Ephraim Faithful " asserted
that unbelief would make for injustice, tyranny and fraud.
He deplored the anti-Christian tendency of his age and felt
that only by rejecting skepticism could a country be prosperous and liberty achieved.[30]

From a literary viewpoint, deistic thought was less in

[29] T. Clap, *Essay on the Nature, etc.*, pp. 41, 47, 53.

[30] *The American Magazine*, January, 1745, pp. 21-2; September, 1746,
p. 404.

evidence in the Middle Provinces than in New England; what little did prevail here was chiefly expressed in newspaper or magazine articles. The Middle Colonies generally accepted the idea of toleration and, except in New York, no serious efforts were made to establish any one church. Even there the attempt failed because the great majority of people belonged to churches other than the Anglican. Thus, a spirit of live and let live had to be adopted and liberty of conscience was extended to all but " papists ". The Catholics were discriminated against not only in New York but also in Pennsylvania. Besides Anglicans and Catholics, there were in the Middle Colonies Quakers, Mennonites, Moravians, Lutherans and Calvinists. The last group included members of the Dutch Reformed, Presbyterian and German Reformed Churches and was the most important religious element in this section of British America.

In such relatively tolerant surroundings, religious liberalism was certain to raise its head. In the College of Philadelphia (later the University of Pennsylvania), founded by the deistic Franklin, rationalism, free from narrowness, flourished. This institution was headed by a liberal Anglican, William Smith, whose views were similar to those of the English Latitudinarian clergy. In his *General Idea of the College of Mirania* (1753) and in his *Philosophical Meditation, and Religious Address to the Supreme Being* (1754), Smith sought to advance natural and revealed religion. He praised the Deity as a wise and good Parent who had bestowed upon men " the noble Faculties of reason and understanding." These capacities, the Anglican clergyman argued, must be improved because upon their advancement depended the progress of truth and happiness. God desired men not only to better their mental powers but to love Him and His creatures. Such a feeling was inculcated by the teaching of natural religion which Smith urged in order to make young men more receptive to the truth and value of Christianity. He likewise suggested a closer examination of revealed faith.[31]

Over King's College in New York (later Columbia University) presided Samuel Johnson who in his youth entertained practically the same views as William Smith. In 1714, while a student at Yale, he heard that a new philosophy was in vogue and that Descartes, Boyle, Locke and Newton were its prophets. He was, however, warned to shun the new metaphysics because it was bound to bring in " a new divinity and corrupt the pure religion of the country. . . ." After his graduation, Johnson became a tutor at Yale where his most celebrated pupil was Jonathan Edwards. Forced to resign from the college in 1720 because of his " incompetence " as a teacher, he became pastor of a church in West Haven and thus was near enough to his Alma Mater to continue his studies. Meanwhile, he was reading the works of prominent Anglican clergymen and was beginning to doubt the validity of his Congregational ordination. By 1722, he determined to cross the Atlantic and take orders in the Anglican Church. In England, Johnson came in contact with the leading Anglican prelates and visited prominent places of interest.[32] He eventually became an Anglican minister and was satisfied that in this church he had found learning, order and urbanity.

In his youth, Johnson was receptive to the ideas of Locke, Newton and such milder English deists as Wollaston whose *Religion of Nature,* although well meant, was "a great stumbling block to many. . . ." It was Collins's *Discourse of the Grounds and Reasons of the Christian Religion* which

[31] W. Smith, *Discourses on Public Occasions in America,* pp. 45, 88-9, 101, 149, 152-5 (Appendix).

[32] S. Johnson, *His Career and Writings,* ed. H. and C. Schneider (New York, 1929), vol. i, pp. 6, 11-2, 15, 17-8.

encouraged the future college president to examine the evidences of Christianity. From this examination, Johnson emerged a good Christian who viewed with sorrow the " deplorable progress of infidelity " from " the well meaning but too conceited Mr. Locke, down to Tindal, and thence to Bolingbroke, etc. etc." [33] Although he observed during his lifetime that Latitudinarianism led to deism and deism to atheism, this did not prevent him from espousing Latitudinarian views. He was convinced that no conflict existed between the new science and older revealed truths; and therefore accepted, like Tillotson, the tenets of natural religion and the divine origin of the Christian revelation. In a sermon, delivered at Stratford, September 7, 1727, he illustrated the need of Christianity by arguing that " the light of nature " was insufficient and consequently he urged that reason be supplemented by divine revelation which taught the average man just ideas concerning God. Of all supernatural disclosures the truest was that of Christianity which was fortified by an excellent system of morality and was attested by miracles and prophecies.[34] Some sixteen years later, in his *Introduction to the Study of Philosophy,* Johnson likewise urged men to accept the Bible as an aid to " mere unassisted reason. . . ." Although insufficient, the rational was nevertheless to be used " to find out and know the Truth. . . ." Real happiness depended upon the cultivation of " right Reason " which was to guide one in the practice of virtue. The good life consisted in promoting individual and public welfare. Moreover, he believed that personal conduct determined the position each man would enjoy in the future world. His views as to immortality were naturally based on the assumption that God existed.[35]

[33] *Ibid.*, vol. i, p. 23.

[34] S. Johnson, *The Necessity of Reveal'd Religion* (MS.), pp. 6-12, 15.

[35] S. Johnson, *Introduction to the Study of Philosophy*, pp. 5-7, 20, 25.

Although the stand of Johnson in his youth was rather liberal and heterodox, by the time he became president of the New York seat of learning, his position was extremely conservative and orthodox. Playing a prominent role in the establishment of King's College was William Livingston who did all in his power to liberalize the new institution. Graduating from Yale at the head of his class in 1741, Livingston came to New York to practice law. When the Anglican Church attempted to gain control of the newly proposed college, he threw himself into the battle. Opposing sectarian education, a limited curriculum and a privately supported institution, he suggested that the college be established by an act of the legislature. This body was to be given the power of appointing trustees who in turn were to elect a president. Although not completely victorious, the young lawyer had the satisfaction of seeing a governing board appointed representing other denominations besides the Anglican. In the meantime, he became editor of a magazine, *The Independent Reflector* (1752), whose articles on religion so aroused the enmity of the clergy that Livingston was described as an atheist and deist. The future Governor of New Jersey merited neither of these titles; he was far from being an atheist since he believed in the existence of a Deity and as for being a deist his acceptance of the Christian revelation precluded that possibility.[36] On the whole, his religious views were liberal; he opposed intolerance and thought that a man might be a good Christian without belonging to any denominational church. He believed sincerely in the divine authority of Christianity but urged that it be freely investigated. If religion was to mean anything, it must be simple, plain and intelligible and con-

---

[36] In later life he published a satirical magazine article in which he ridiculed deism. See chapter iv, pp. 107-8 and Sedgwick, *A Memoir of the Life of William Livingston* (New York, 1833), p. 249 (note).

sequently was to be purged of all superstitious accretions and priestly inventions.[37]

Naturally Livingston encountered the opposition of the Anglican party in New York and soon his friends began to forsake him. Among the latter was James Parker who refused to support *The Independent Reflector* because he feared the loss of the government's printing business. Besides, in 1752, Parker found himself assailed by the orthodox of the city for an allegorical article published in his newspaper. In this composition, some Indian chiefs were used to popularize deistic principles. According to the account, a Swedish missionary, attempting to convert some Red Men in 1710, asserted that the Deity had revealed Himself in the Bible and that if the Scriptures were not accepted, eternal damnation would follow. In reply, the Indians stated that future rewards and punishments were allotted in proportion to the good or evil that was done in this life. They held that this idea had been disclosed to their forefathers or implanted in their own natures. Moreover, they argued that the supernatural testimony of Christianity had no advantage over their own because the Supreme Being had the power to reveal Himself to all men without the aid of any book. Any religion, teaching a special revelation, was blasphemous, since it represented the Deity as a tyrant who capriciously condemned most of His creatures to eternal misery, although they were not at fault. Even if the Bible were of divine origin, the Indians were thankful that God had not forced it upon them. In conclusion, they prayed to be saved from certain conceptions set forth in it.

That this speech was an implied rejection of the Christian revelation was so obvious that it was immediately answered by a defender of the faith. In a letter to the newspaper, an

[37] Sedgwick, *op. cit.*, pp. 55, 75-6, 86-7; and Richardson, *A History of Early American Magazines*, pp. 83-5, 89.

anonymous correspondent pointed out that the Swedish missionary was not represented " as a faithful minister of Christ " and that therefore the narrative was most misleading.   Yet, he left the entire controversy " to our able Divines, who were better able . . . to take the Author of the Paper to Task, about some impious Expressions in the conclusion." In a footnote to the above broadside, the editor, James Parker, stated that he meant no harm and had only desired to give the adversaries of Christianity a fair hearing.   This statement, however, did not satisfy the faithful and Parker was forced to call upon Franklin for aid.   Later, he publicly apologized for his " impious work " and appeased the orthodox by asserting his belief in the Trinity.[38]

Playing a part in the Parker episode was Cadwallader Colden, a prolific writer and tireless student who had few peers in the intellectual circles of provincial America. Franklin wrote to him in behalf of the persecuted printer and as usual approached just the right man for the business at hand since Colden was not only influential in New York politics but was also somewhat of a skeptic himself.   In his *Explication of the First Causes of Action in Matter and of the Cause of Gravitation,* he showed himself to be a materialist whose position was dangerously close to atheism.   The treatise, though exciting much discussion in Europe, hardly made a ripple here; on the whole, it illustrated a combination of erudition and originality and was an attempted criticism of an enlargement upon the work of Newton.   To Colden, there were three kinds of matter: (1) the resisting force opposing or suppressing motion; (2) the self-moving power always ready to change or endeavor to change its position; and (3) the elastic or expansive force reflecting or conveying

[38] *The New-York Gazette revived in the Weekly Post-Boy,* April 27, 1752 (no. 484) ; May 4, 1752 (no. 485) ; and August 3, 1752 (No. 498). See also B. Franklin, *Writings,* ed. Smyth, vol. iii, pp. 87-8.

any action from an agent.   None of these three "species" of matter had within it the power to attract any other. Apparent attraction or gravitation was performed by "pulsion" which was the result of the joint actions of the resisting, moving and elastic powers.[39]   This was an enlargement upon the work of Newton, who, according to Colden, did not in his writings attribute an attractive force to matter but merely spoke of an apparent gravitation, the perpetual effect of a cause of which he was ignorant.   By implying that motion was inherent in matter, Colden was philosophically close to the atheistic contention that a First Cause was not needed to give the heavenly bodies their initial thrust. Yet, the future lieutenant-governor of New York explicitly denied this implication by asserting that some Intelligent Being was needed to create the celestial objects as well as to give them distinct kinds of motion.   As to the problem of right and wrong, Colden was convinced that men had the power to follow their inclinations.   Naturally they were responsible for their actions.   Morality, he held, consisted in so living one's life as to achieve happiness.

According to observers, deism was making rapid headway in the Middle Colonies.   In a Philadelphia newspaper, *The American Weekly Museum,* October 9-16, 1735 (no. 824), an article appeared lamenting the fact that skepticism was meeting with encouragement and was especially poisoning young minds.   Had the readers of this Philadelphia journal taken the trouble to look about them, they would have found that deism had already "poisoned" more mature minds. On one of his visits to the city of brotherly love, the renowned evangelist, the Reverend Mr. Whitefield, preached a sermon which melted the hearts of some of the "most marvellous Offenders against the Great God."   Among the

---

[39] Colden, *An Explication of the First Causes of Action in Matter and the Cause of Gravitation* (New York, 1746), pp. 21-2, 33, 51.

latter was a "notorious deist", Brockden, a recorder of
deeds, who was then sixty years of age and who had throughout his life zealously attempted to propagate deistical principles among "moral Men". Prevailed upon by another
deist, Brockden had consented to attend Whitefield's meeting. He came, he saw and was conquered! [40] Philadelphia
apparently had quite a number of deists because on another
occasion Whitefield addressed a gathering of "Reasoning
unbelievers" who were far from impressed by his attacks
upon natural reason. At about this time, another clergyman, Jonathan Dickinson, noted that frequenters of inns and
coffee houses were indulging in skeptical conversations. In
a letter, dated 1764, Franklin pertinently remarked to one
of his cynical friends, " . . . If you had Christian Faith,
quantum suff., [a proof of immortality] might not be necessary, but as matters are, it may be of some Use." [41] In
the meantime, apologists were endeavoring to check the
progress of deism by vindicating the truth of the Christian
revelation. In 1732, Jonathan Dickinson, later president of
the College of New Jersey, published a work, *The Reasonableness of Christianity*, designed to prove that Jesus was
the divine Messiah and son of God and that no religion
except his own could be attested by miracles. Although
Dickinson allowed for the sake of argument that "the
Patrons of Infidelity" could produce the "fabulous Histories" of Mohammed and the "infamous legends" of the
Popes, he claimed that these stories were merely "the bare
reports of . . . unknown Authors. . . ." Furthermore, he

40 Whitefield, *A Continuation of the Rev. Mr. Whitefield's Journal,*
etc. (London, 1744), pp. 66-7.

41 J. Dickinson, *Familiar Letters* (Glasgow, 1775), p. 2; B. Franklin,
Writings, ed. Smyth, vol. iv, p. 250 (Letter to William Strahan, June 25,
1764).

challenged the deists to draw up a system which could explain man's lost innocency and which could keep man submissive.[42]

Some thirteen years later, Dickinson returned to the counter-attack in his *Familiar Letters upon a Variety of Religious Subjects.* In this pamphlet, he asserted that even the deists were forced to admit that the religion of Jesus was worthy both of God and man. To prove that it was revealed by the Deity, this " great Divine, who was not much of a Scholar ", as Ezra Stiles put it, showed that Christ had fulfilled the Hebraic prophecies, that he had performed miracles, and that he had given to the world a practical morality.[43] Dickinson was aided in his defence of Christianity by magazine contributors. In a Philadelphia periodical, a correspondent defended the excellence of the gospel, the superiority of Christianity and the existence of a miracle-working Providence.[44] In another issue of the same magazine, there appeared a communication from a clergyman who pointed out that all followers of Christianity were assured of eternal salvation. Later a writer, commenting on this letter, observed that the death of " the very feeblest of true Christians " was superior even to that of a Socrates.[45] In a similar vein, " Publicola ", in a Woodbridge (New Jersey) periodical, *The New American Magazine,* August 1758 (no. 8), informed his readers that while the religious man had little to lose if his faith were built on weak grounds, the " infidel " had everything to forfeit, if he were wrong.

[42] J. Dickinson, *Reasonableness of Christianity,* pp. 54, 78-85, 95, 100-1, 106, 120-1, 160-1.

[43] J. Dickinson, *Familiar Letters, etc.,* pp. 11-16.

[44] *The American Magazine and Monthly Chronicle for the British Colonies,* March, 1758 and September, 1758 (nos. 6 and 12), vol. i, pp. 290, 331, 600-2.

[45] *Ibid.,* March, 1758 and April, 1759 (nos. 6 and 7), vol. i, pp. 291-4, 331.

In the South, the deistic movement was still less conspicuous than in the North. Here the Church of England was established by law and, except in North Carolina, the Establishment was fairly effective. Taking the provincial period as a whole, the Anglican Church lost ground as compared with the Dissenters, of whom the strongest and most aggressive were the Presbyterians. The latter were to be found chiefly in the back country and, although intensely partisan, their contact on the frontier with peoples of different denominations gradually developed in them a spirit of toleration. During this period, the Anglican Church in Virginia, although outwardly prosperous, was considerably weakened. This was due to a steady increase in the number of Dissenters, the spiritual laxity of the clergy and the exaction of clerical salaries. Hostility to the clergy flared up in the famous Parson's Cause (1755-1758) occasioned by an act of the assembly providing for the payment of church taxes in money, instead of tobacco, at a rate below the market value. The clergy protested and failing to get relief in Virginia, appealed to the King who annulled the objectionable law. To test whether the royal order affected salaries payable between the passage of the act and its repeal, a case was made in which Patrick Henry, retained by the parishioners, practically secured a favorable decision. During the trial, young Henry, though a member of the Anglican Church, made a violent attack upon its clergy.

Yet, in spite of this incident, up to 1763, a vigorous anticlerical movement was lacking in Virginia. In the absence of such a tendency and in the presence of a general indifference to theological speculations, deism had little chance to gain ground. According to Bishop Meade, the lay readers of the Anglican Church used none but Tillotson's sermons.[46]

---

[46] Meade, *Old Churches, etc.*, vol. ii, p. 355.

These discourses, generally cold and unanimated, dealt with "moral virtues" and were not calculated to stir the heart. In 1722, James Blair, president of William and Mary College, stated that the Anglican ministry of Virginia had "little occasion in [their] sermons to enter the lists with Atheists, Deists . . ." etc. because the colony was not "infested with the enemies of the Christian faith. . . ." [47] At about this time, Sir John Randolph of Williamsburg was being reproached by his friends because of reputed deistic ideas. Sir John, however, was far from being a deist; in fact, in his will, he made a public profession of faith to the contrary. He believed that Christ was born miraculously and came into the world to persuade men to love their neighbors. He was convinced that people would be judged in the future world by the life they led rather than by mistakes in matters of speculation. In conclusion, Randolph condemned "learned Doctors" for striving to make the religion of Jesus a religion of "mysteries".[48] The unpopularity of deistic speculation in the South was also reflected in newspaper articles. In the *Maryland Gazette* for November 22-29, 1734 (no. 90), an anonymous writer attempted to prove that the action of God, in commanding the sacrifice of Isaac, was consistent with His character. The correspondent argued that the narrative furnished an example of faith and obedience as well as a prediction of the future life of the Saviour. Moreover, in answer to the deistic contention that Abraham was acting contrary to natural law in attempting to kill his son, the writer held that the Patriarch was motivated to do what he did by reasonable and moral considerations and consequently his actions were justifiable.

[47] Quoted in the *History of the College of William and Mary from its Foundation, 1660 to 1874* (Richmond, 1874), p. 45.

[48] *General Magazine and Historical Chronicle*, May, 1741, vol. i, pp. 346-7.

In North Carolina, a general indifference, if not hostility, to organized religion prevailed. In Edenton, a town on the north side of Albemarle Sound, Colonel Byrd of Virginia was surprised to find neither a church nor a place of public worship.[49] He discovered that the people here were opposed to priests, christening ceremonies and sermons. In a similar fashion, the celebrated Wesley, who came to America to convert Indians and returned to England with the realization that he needed conversion, found that the people of Frederica, near Savannah, Georgia, were " cold and heartless . . ." to religious concerns. Yet, even more distressing to the famous founder of Methodism was the appearance of deists in Georgia. On May 18, 1737, Wesley discovered, as he believed, "the first Convert to Deism " made in Savannah. At first this unnamed skeptic had been " zealously and examplarily religious " but unfortunately soon lost both zeal and faith. Thereafter, others followed with such rapidity that by September of the same year, Wesley was forced to read to his congregation a number of sermons with the hope that these might prove " a timely Antidote against the Poison of Infidelity, which was now with great Industry propagated among us. . . ." His fears for the safety of Georgia became so pronounced that he felt called upon to state in his *Journal* that deism was more dangerous to the existence of the new colony than Catholicism.[50]

[49] The construction of St. Paul's Church, Edenton, was begun eight years after Byrd's observation. Although work was started on the edifice in 1736, it was not until 1760 that church services were held in the building for the first time. By 1774, the church was finished at an estimated cost of $25,000 to $30,000. (*North Carolina Historical and Genealogical Register* (Edenton, 1900), vol. i, pp. 608-9.)

[50] J. Wesley, *An Extract of the Reverend Mr. John Wesley's Journal, etc.* (Bristol, 1739 [?]), pp. 32, 35, 41-2, 53.

CHAPTER IV

DEISM IN REVOLUTIONARY AMERICA (1763-1789)

FROM 1763 to 1789, the section north of the Mason and Dixon line made great progress in the matter of " soul freedom "; but religious discrimination of one kind or another still persisted. The Massachusetts state constitution required the governor to declare himself a supporter of the Christian religion, and though every citizen could claim the right to worship as he pleased, equal protection under the law was limited to Christians. Likewise Massachusetts practically excluded Catholics from holding office. In Pennsylvania, much to the disgust of the deistic Franklin, the state constitution required all legislators to declare their belief in the divine inspiration of the Bible. Moreover, state churches still persisted in New England; the Massachusetts constitution compelled each town to support " public Protestant teachers " and required its citizens to pay taxes for the support of some kind of Protestant service. According to this provision, if Baptists, Quakers and others maintained their own churches, they were not forced to support the Congregational Establishment. In Connecticut, a general toleration act was passed in 1784 which allowed every religious body to manage its own affairs. To this provision, however, was affixed the condition that all Dissenters, desiring exemption from the payment of Congregational taxes, were required to produce certificates to the effect that they were supporting their respective denominations. These were granted by church and civil officials with the result that many times Baptists, Quakers, Anglicans and others were forced to support the Establishment or suffer the punishment of imprisonment or fine.

Yet, in spite of these discriminations, toleration was more prevalent in the North than at any previous time. Amid these more tolerant surroundings, religious liberalism made rapid progress. In New England, the Unitarian tendency was making such an appeal that, according to one exaggerated observation, it was unfashionable to discuss the divinity of Christ because the subject was considered antiquated. Boston, Cambridge and Salem were the principal centers of the anti-Trinitarian movement. In 1767, Simeon Howard, succeeding Mayhew as minister of West Church, Boston, rejected the doctrines of the Trinity, predestination and the total depravity of man. Some eighteen years later, under the guidance of James Freeman, a reader in the Anglican Church, King's Chapel revised its Prayer Book in order to strike out any references to Trinitarian beliefs. Influenced greatly by William Hazlitt, an English Unitarian, who was then visiting Boston, Freeman believed that Christ, although not a member of the Godhead, was still more than a man and consequently, he addressed Jesus as his Saviour and Redeemer. Joseph Willard, President of Harvard, also showed Unitarian tendencies and was in constant communication with such English leaders as Priestley and Price. At Salem, worldly-wise merchants engaged in the East Indian trade listened approvingly to the liberal doctrines of the Reverend William Bentley. Out of Salem's twenty-four most prominent families twenty were Unitarians. Commercial contacts with the Orient probably made these families receptive to latitudinarian ideas in religion. At least, their minister was quite liberal in his views. Although not a deist, Bentley circulated deistic works. On one occasion, he lent Tindal's *Christianity as Old as the Creation* to a friend who promised to read it in private. It was left under his pillow, was discovered by a woman who gave it to an aunt, who, in turn, read it to her husband. Although himself a believer in the Christian revelation, Bentley was willing to admit that anyone who sincerely thought that Christianity was wrong honored God by rejecting it. In 1790, he preached a sermon at Stone Chapel, Boston, in which he rejected the Calvinistic doctrine of special election and upheld the excellence of natural religion. To him, all men were, and always had been, capable of attaining salvation and happiness. Furthermore Bentley held that " the honest devotion of a heathen" was more acceptable to God than "the hypocrisy of a Christian". The "most excellent religion" was that of nature which consisted in doing the will of God and which was revealed to man through the dictates of reason. Christianity was not to be considered as an enemy to natural religion but rather a supplement to it.[1]

Universalism, like Unitarianism, was beginning to gain ground in the North. During the Revolutionary period, both Universalists and Unitarians believed that it was the purpose of God to save all men irrespective of creed, but, whereas the Unitarians rejected the doctrine of the Trinity, the Universalists generally expressed no opinion as to the equality or subordination of Jesus to God. After 1805, however, most of the Universalist ministry publicly defended anti-Trinitarian beliefs.[2] The leading Universalists of the period were John Murray and Elhanan Winchester. John Murray, an Englishman who came to America in 1770, promoted the rise of Universalism. In 1774, he was drawn to the town of Gloucester, Massachusetts, because of the religious sentiments of its inhabitants. Unlike some other Uni-

---

[1] Allen and Eddy, *History of the Unitarians and Universalists in the U. S.* (New York, 1894), pp. 180-5; Cooke, *Unitarianism in America* (Boston, 1902), pp. 66, 71-2, 76-9; W. Bentley, *Diary* (Salem, 1905), vol. i, p. 98, *A Sermon Preached at Stone Chapel in Boston, September 12, 1790* (Boston, 1790), pp. 8-9, 11, 15, 17; and Schneider, *The Puritan Mind*, pp. 204-6.

[2] Allen and Eddy, *op. cit.*, p. 429.

versalists of his time, he did not believe in future punishments since the evil that men did in this life was washed away by their belief in Christ who died for all.   Among the early Universalists, the most eminent for learning and intellect was a former Baptist clergyman, Elhanan Winchester.   In 1780, there was division in the ranks of his church in Philadelphia, and the following year he organized his dissenting brethren under the name of the Society of Universal Baptists.   In his dialogues on *Universal Restoration* (1792), Winchester interpreted the Bible so broadly that its passages seemed to prove his contention that all men would be ultimately saved. He based his doctrine of restoration on the principles that " God [was] the universal and only creator . . .", that He was benevolent, and that His Son had died for all.   In 1789, the Universalists of Philadelphia, over whom Winchester pre-sided, addressed a letter to friendly societies asking them to meet in convention.   This gathering met the following year and drew up certain articles of faith.   Among these was a belief in the divine inspiration of the Bible, in the existence of one God, and in the salvation of all men through the death of Christ.[3]

Religious liberalism in the North appeared not only in the form of Unitarianism and Universalism but also of deism. From 1763 to 1789, the deistic movement became more significant than ever before and although still essentially moderate in speculation, it showed an increasing militancy. Fundamental to deistic thought was the idea of a general Providence which operated in accordance with universal laws.   A corollary naturally deduced from this basic assumption was the inference that if God ruled the world according to general edicts, He would not go out of His

[3] Allen and Eddy, *op. cit.*, pp. 388, 390, 394-5, 405, 407-9, 414, 420-1; E. Winchester, *The Universal Restoration* (Bellows Falls, Vt., 1819), pp. 119-123; and Cooke, *op. cit.*, pp. 67-9.

way to reveal Himself to any particular people through such supernatural events as miracles. In June 1769, a Philadelphia periodical, *The American Magazine, or General Repository,* published a letter defending this deistic contention. The author argued that since worldly evils might all be for the best, man had little need of any particular intervention by an external Being. Reflecting the liberal revolutionary spirit of the age, the writer asked, " Why then should God interpose to alter the determinations of human will, more than the operations of nature? Cannot man be happy unless his liberty be over-ruled? " Furthermore, evidences of any intervention were merely assertions and although such events might have taken place, there were no criteria to judge of their wisdom or foolishness. In conclusion, the writer cautiously stated that what he had said did not preclude the possibility that if the Deity desired to reveal Himself by suspending His general edicts, He could do so. That the letter was an implied rejection of revelation was so evident that it was immediately answered. In the August 1769 issue of the same periodical, a " particular Providence " was defended on the ground that, since the Deity cared equally for all His children and disposed of all events, such foresight did not imply any partiality on His part. In subsequent issues, the original contributor defended his thesis and re-affirmed his faith in a general Providence and free will.[4] Since it was the policy of Lewis Nicola, curator of the American Philosophical Society and editor of the *American Magazine, or General Repository,* to publish nothing " derogtory to the principles of the Christian religion ", other articles did not evoke much controversy.

About this time, Nathaniel Ames, moved by anti-clerical feeling, indulged in the deistic phraseology of his time and

[4] *The American Magazine or General Repository,* June, 1769, August, 1769, September, 1769, pp. 174-7, 237-42, 304-6.

although not definitely a deist, was distinctly liberal in religion. To this publisher of almanacs, true religion was the essence of correct reason, while morality was the vital spark of all faith. Moreover, "to defend the Christian religion [was] one thing and to knock a man on the head . . ." for disbelieving in it would be another. Furthermore, hypocrisy generally flourished under the guise of orthodoxy. Another printer, Theophilus Cossart, a German, was regarded by his contemporaries as "a Freethinker and Philosopher . . .", who believed in the existence of God and a future state. According to Ezra Stiles, Cossart thought that "the Morals of the Mohametans [were] superior to those of the Christians in general"—a favorite argument employed by deists to indicate their dislike for Christianity. Having resided at one time or another in Charleston, Philadelphia, New York, Newport and Boston, the German printer had an excellent opportunity to spread his heterodox views.[5]

While deists were declaring their independence from a miracle-working Deity, the thirteen American colonies were doing the same in reference to England. At the outbreak of the struggle, deism was still a cult limited to a few members of the intellectual classes residing in relatively large towns. Outside of these cities it was scarcely known; in fact, John Leland, a Baptist clergyman who was then living in a small village only forty miles from Boston, observed that he had never heard of "Deism and Universalism . . . and of course was what is called a believer in revelation." If, by chance, the deistic philosophy made its way into the interior, it was certain to be regarded with a great deal of suspicion. On the eve of the Revolution, Joseph Clarke of Northampton requested Henry Knox, a Boston bookseller,

[5] N. Ames, *Essays, Humor, and Poems, with Notes and Comments* by S. Briggs (Cleveland, 1891), pp. 387, 403, and Stiles, *Diary*, ed. Dexter, vol. i, pp. 179-80.

to send him Hume's *Essays* and Leland's *Views of Deistical Writers*. Clarke urged his dealer to take every precaution to insure secrecy and directed Knox to deliver the books to a Mr. Smith. Since the latter proceeded to Boston a little too early, the purchase was not made. Fearing that Knox might send the books by another messenger, Clarke instructed the Bostonian not to dispatch them until Smith again visited the city. The prospective buyer explained that he was forced to adopt such measures because of the " bigoted attachment of the people in this part of the country to the particular principles in Religion that they had been educated in . . ." and because of " the Infamy they would Cast upon any man who differed from them in so material a point, as they would readily conclude he did, were he known to be possessed of books on Theism. . . ." [6]

The unpopularity of deism was also reflected in the actions of the Pennsylvania Convention of 1776 called to draw up a state constitution. The deistic Franklin, who presided, was apparently unable to stop the Convention from incorporating a constitutional provision stating that every representative was to declare his belief in the divine inspiration of the Bible. Some eight years later, in a letter to Priestley, the English Unitarian, Franklin told of his opposition to the above clause and felt called upon to remark that there were " several Things in the Old Testament impossible to be given by divine Inspiration. . . ." [7] Since no vote was recorded on this constitutional provision, it is impossible to say how the delegates stood. Probably the Scotch-Irish of the interior favored the clause because of their conservative religious views. William Findley, who could have been easily elected to the convention had he wished it, typified

[6] Massachusetts Historical Society *Proceedings* (Boston, 1928), vol. lxi, pp. 250-1, 259-60.

[7] Franklin, *Writings,* ed. Smyth, vol. ix, pp. 266-7.

the religious conservatism of these God-fearing Presbyterians. A deeply pious individual, he was a bitter opponent of deism. The piety of the Pennsylvania Convention was further displayed in the passage of a resolution providing for the initiation of divine services in order to praise "Almighty God . . . for the peculiar interposition of his special providence. . . ." [8]

In the same year that the Pennsylvania Convention met to write a state constitution, the American colonies in Congress assembled announced their freedom from England. Though the majority of those who signed the Declaration of Independence were agreed as to the desirableness of " soul freedom ", their views on other religious questions were so diversified that they ran the gamut from the deism of Jefferson to the orthodoxy of Sherman. The author has examined the religious opinions of a little more than a third of the fifty-six delegates who affixed their signatures to the document. Of these, three were deists, two showed distinct deistic leanings, four entertained liberal, though not deistic, views, while the remaining eleven were definitely orthodox in their principles. Benjamin Franklin of Pennsylvania, Thomas Jefferson of Virginia, and Stephen Hopkins of Rhode Island espoused more or less openly the cause of deism, while John Adams of Massachusetts [9] and George

[8] Channing, *History of the United States* (New York, 1924), vol. iii, pp. 438-9; *Proceedings Relative to the Calling of the Conventions of 1776 and 1790 ... With a View of the Proceedings of the Convention of 1776* (Harrisburg, 1825), pp. 46-7, 53 (note), 58. Biographical sketches of the Cumberland, Westmoreland and Berks County delegation can be found in McMaster and Stone, *Pennsylvania and the Federal Constitution* (Lancaster, 1888), pp. 733, 735; Albert, *History of the County of Westmoreland, Pa.* (Philadelphia, 1882), pp. 78-9 (note) ; and Montgomery, *History of Berks County, Pa.* (Reading, 1894), pp. 223-4, 232-3, 235-6, 237-8, 247-50.

[9] For the deistic views of Franklin see chapter iii, pp. 63-7 ; for those of Jefferson chapter iv, pp. 116-7; for those of Hopkins chapter iv, p. 105; and for the deistic inclinations of Adams chapter iii, p. 68 and chapter v, pp. 141-2.

Wythe of Virginia, were close to the deistic philosophy. Wythe of the Old Dominion (1726-1806) was a friend of Jefferson and a professor of law at William and Mary. On the subject of religion he was strangely silent because, according to Jefferson, he was afraid to trust anyone with so important a matter. His contemporaries suspected him of "infidelity". So prevalent was this suspicion that when Wythe died, his friend, William Munford, stated publicly that the former professor was a believer in the truth of the Christian religion and that before his death he " ' often prayed to Jesus Christ his Saviour, for relief ' " [10] Significantly enough, Munford mentioned that Wythe had informed him of his acceptance of the validity of Christianity only one or two years before his death. Robert T. Paine, Josiah Bartlett, Benjamin Rush and Matthew Thornton held liberal religious views. Robert Treat Paine of Massachusetts (1731-1814) was the son of a minister and in his youth received "the best moral and religious instruction". He was interested in theological matters and occasionally preached. Paine regarded Christianity as a system of moral truths and righteousness given by God to man. His approach to the question of religion was practical; he thought that if Christianity did not make men virtuous, it was of no benefit. Like Paine, Bartlett (1729-1795) was a liberal in religion. The future governor of New Hampshire, while still a young man, was given the opportunity of using the library of a liberal clergymen of Salisbury, the Reverend Dr. Webster. He soon came to doubt the traditional doctrines of Calvinism and during the greater part of his life, believed that man was free to do as he pleased but was to be held responsible for his actions. By profession Bartlett was a doctor of medicine but in this field he was less widely

[10] J. Sanderson (ed.), *Biography of the Signers to the Declaration of Independence* (Philadelphia, 1823), vol. ii, pp. 180-1, 184.

known than Benjamin Rush of Pennsylvania (1745-1813), friend of Franklin and Jefferson. The Virginian carried on quite a correspondence with the Philadelphia physician and often exchanged with the latter his advanced religious views probably with the thought that Rush would understand and be sympathetic towards them. The doctor, however, was not a deist; in fact, *The Age of Reason* was so repugnant to his principles that he showed no desire to renew his friendship with Paine upon the latter's return to the United States. In short, the scientist was a Christian who revered the Bible, urged the excellency of Christianity and attended church. Like Rush, Thornton of New Hampshire (c. 1741-1803) was a physician and a religious liberal. He refused to affiliate himself with any religious denomination, believed in the existence of God, accepted the divine mission of Christ and, in short, would have classed himself as a Christian.[11]

Along with Livingston, Jefferson, Adams and Franklin, Roger Sherman was a member of the committee appointed to draw up the Declaration of Independence. Sherman of Connecticut (1721-1793) did not have much of a formal education but attained as a result of his own industry a considerable knowledge of science, law and theology. According to the testimony of his friend, Dr. Jonathan Edwards the younger, Sherman was an excellent theologian. Upon one occasion he argued a fine theological point with the renowned Reverend Samuel Hopkins on the theory of " disinterested submission ". Sherman held that men would not be willing to give up their " eternal interest " of salvation for the glory of God and the good of man. The Connecticut statesman believed in the Bible as the revealed word of God, in the fall of man and his consequent sinfulness and in the final day of judgment when the bad would be sentenced to

[11] Sanderson (ed.), *op. cit.*, vol. ii, pp. 211-4, 244-5; vol. iii, pp. 136-7; vol. iv, p. 283; and vol. v, p. 67.

everlasting punishment and the good would be rewarded with eternal life. Although tolerant of differences in religious matters, Sherman intensely disliked "irreligious" men. He opposed the confirmation of Morris as minister to France because he objected to Morris' practice " of speaking irreverently of the Christian religion. . . ." Like Sherman, his colleague, Oliver Scott (1726-1797), was deeply orthodox but at the same time tolerant in his religious views. According to one biographer, the future governor of Connecticut was pure in morals and faith; he was a " humble christian, untainted by bigotry or intolerance." William Williams (1731-1811), another Connecticut man, was likewise rigidly orthodox in his principles and yet was a firm believer in religious liberty. A member of the Congregational order, a deacon from his youth to his death, Williams attended church regularly and contributed money to missionary societies designed to spread Gospel teachings. Richard Stockton of New Jersey (1730-1781) was also tolerant of the opinion of others, although he himself was a strict Calvinist. He subscribed to the doctrine of human depravity and exhorted his children to remember that the fear of God was the beginning of wisdom. Carter Braxton of Virginia (1736-1797) advocated likewise the cause of religious liberty. Educated at William and Mary, he was an intelligent man who, while favoring independence from England, feared the democratic " ravings " of a goodly number of Americans. In 1785, he supported the cause of " soul freedom " in the Old Dominion in spite of the fact that he was an active churchman. Like Braxton, Francis Hopkinson of Pennsylvania (1737-1791) was an Anglican who was interested in ecclesiastical matters. In 1789, he served as secretary of a convention of the Episcopal Church. Samuel Huntington, Philip Livingston, John Witherspoon, Abraham Clark and James Smith were all orthodox Christians. Huntington (1732-1796), destined to become governor of Connecticut, was a " friend " of religion and a " member of the Christian Church ". His faith in Christian principles was said to have been unshaken and he was accustomed to preach sermons on them. Like Huntington, Livingston of New York (1716-1778) was " a firm believer in the sublime truths of religion, and a humble follower of our divine Saviour." Witherspoon (1722-1794), President of Princeton, was a strict Presbyterian divine whose orthodoxy was unquestioned. His colleague from New Jersey, Clark (1726-1794), was also a devout Presbyterian, while Smith of Pennsylvania (c. 1713-1800), although inclined to joke, never allowed himself to utter a witty remark at the expense of religion or the clergy.[12]

Differences as to religious opinions prevailed not only among the signers of the Declaration of Independence but also among other Revolutionary leaders. Willie Jones, a member of the Continental Congress from North Carolina, Edmund Randolph, a prominent Virginian statesman, Ethan Allen, hero of Ticonderoga and Thomas Paine, writer of *Common Sense* rejected either implicitly or explicitly the Christian revelation. Even though George Washington, James Madison and George Mason did not go so far, their views on religion were distinctly liberal. On the other hand, Samuel Adams, Patrick Henry and Henry Laurens were religious conservatives. A Puritan of the Puritans, Samuel Adams desired the good people of Boston to follow in the paths of Bradford, Winthrop and other early New England worthies. He also urged that the state should carefully supervise the morals of its people. Moreover, in line with his Puritan heritage, Adams showed himself most hostile

---

[12] Sanderson (ed.), *op. cit.*, vol. iii, pp. 77, 109-10, 114, 192, 290-1, 306; vol. iv, pp. 104-5, 126-7; vol. vii. pp. 182, 235; *Dictionary of American Biography*, vol. ii, pp. 609-10; vol. iv, p. 119; vol. ix, p. 222; and Boutell, *The Life of Roger Sherman* (Chicago, 1896), pp. 271-3, 275-7, 280.

to Catholicism which he felt was subversive of civil liberty. In 1768, he wrote a series of articles for a Boston newspaper in which he suggested that the New England towns should stamp out " Popery " (this only ten years before the French Alliance!). That the Bible was divinely revealed and that its miracles were valid were accepted by him without question. Later he pleaded with Paine to abandon so unworthy a cause as deism and suggested that the defender of the Rights of Man direct his talents along other lines than those of "unchristianizing" good Americans.[13]   Another firm believer in orthodoxy was Patrick Henry who attended church regularly and desired to see religion supported.   The Virginian lawyer was a bitter opponent of freethinking; according to his leading biographer,[14] he was among the few who realized " the undermining influence of French infidelity." To check the progress of deism, Henry printed, in 1789, at his own expense, Soame Jenyns' *View of the Internal Evidences of the Christian Religion,* a book reputed to be anti-deistic.   This work he circulated free of charge particularly among professional people.   Convinced of the truth of Christianity, Henry is said to have written an answer to Paine's *Age of Reason* which, however, he destroyed before his death.   Laurens of South Carolina, merchant, planter and President of the Continental Congress in 1777, was an active member of the Anglican Church who entertained distinctly orthodox views.   He knew the Bible intimately; believed in its divine origin; and required his children to read it.   Yet, Laurens was not a bigot; he was opposed to holding men's consciences in " leading strings."   A liberal

[13] S. Adams, *Writings,* ed. Cushing (New York, 1904), vol. i, pp. 202-3, vol. ii, pp. 269, 271, vol. iii, p. 286, vol. iv, p. 238 and T. Paine, *Writings,* ed. Conway (New York, 1898), vol. iv, pp. 201-2.

[14] W. W. Henry, *Patrick Henry, Life, Correspondence and Speeches* (New York, 1891), vol. ii, p. 200.

in the best sense of the word, he even refused to condemn Voltaire on the ground that he knew too little about the Frenchman.[15]

During the Revolutionary War, Americans came in contact with French soldiers and officers who, according to contemporary New England accounts, were responsible for the spread of a militant freethinking movement. The large majority who came to defend the new Republic were not " without faith and morals ", despite the assertions of pious commentators. Outwardly, at least, the French were religious; they were willing to face the possibility of derision rather than renounce the public celebration of the mass. This sacrament was held in many communities where Catholicism was regarded as " a superstitious and idolatrous religion." Moreover, the men who led the French forces in America were, for the most part, more concerned with military than intellectual pursuits; some of them were old soldiers like Rochambeau, a veteran of the Seven Year's War, or young ones like Count Berthier, later to become Napoleon's chief of staff. The youthful Saint-Simon, destined to be the first great socialist theorist of the coming century, the brilliant Marquis de Chastellux, described by Franklin as " a friend of humanity ", and the scholarly Count de Ségur, the historian, were notable exceptions to the general rule. As was to be expected, some skeptics could be found among the French officers; one of these was de Lauzun whose " sage " observations on philosophy, morality, history and religion so delighted Frederick the Great that the Prussian monarch desired him to remain in Berlin as French ambassador. Whether the skeptical Duke " made " a single American doubt the Christian revelation, as von Steuben " caused " Timothy Pickering to question the Trinity, is

[15] D. D. Wallace, *The Life of Henry Laurens* (New York, 1915), pp. 181, 438-40.

problematic and in the absence of evidence is difficult to ascertain.

The rise of a more intense anti-clerical feeling rather than the " influence " of French culture was responsible for the impetus given to deism after 1783.   In that year, a number of American states had established churches and religious discriminations of one sort or another.   To the advocates of liberalism, it seemed obvious that liberty meant freedom not only from English but from ecclesiastical interference. In order to destroy clerical meddling, they thought it necessary to undermine priestly pretensions to authority.   To achieve this purpose, the deists adopted two methods of approach.   First, most of them endeavored to show that the real teachings of Christ, said to be essentially deistic, were perverted by his followers who substituted for them rituals, creeds and churches.   In turn, these, the deists held, led to bloody struggles within Christendom.   To do away with internal strife, it was necessary to destroy the power of the priesthood and restore the simple teachings of Jesus or, in other words, natural religion.   The second approach, being motivated by a more intense anti-clerical feeling, was by far more militant and attracted fewer supporters.   These men trained their guns of destructive criticism upon the citadel of the Christian revelation upon which rested clerical pretensions to speak authoritatively.   They were convinced that once this fortress fell, the power of the clergy would be forever shattered and the new dispensation begun.

The call for a bolder deism was subtly presented in an article entitled " A Disquisition on Rational Christianity " which appeared in *The Boston Magazine* for 1783. Although the name of the author was not given, it has been definitely established that an Englishman, Soame Jenyns, wrote this pretty little piece.[15]   Jenyns (1704-1787) acquired

---

[16] L. N. Richardson, *History of Early American Magazines*, pp. 218-9.

quite a reputation for himself as a literary figure. In 1776, his *View of the Internal Evidences of the Christian Religion,* which went through ten editions and was translated into several foreign languages, appeared. The exacting Dr. Johnson thought that the work was not very "theological" but the pious Hannah More was happy to note that it was responsible for the conversion of a "philosophical infidel". The book itself called forth a great controversy; some rejoiced that Jenyns had discarded his early skepticism, others, questioning his sincerity, thought that he was still poking fun at the Christian religion. This then was the author whose work *The Boston Magazine* thought fit to reprint. Stripping the Englishman's "Disquisition on Rational Christianity" of its cynicism, the work represented a thrust at the Christian religion. To Jenyns, the Christian drama of salvation appeared " so adverse to all the principles of human reason, that, if brought before her tribunal, it must be inevitably condemned. . . ." Moreover, revelation could not be based on reason because it implied something above the rational. Ironically, the writer held that although various denominational churches could be represented as Christian, rationalists did not deserve this designation because they rejected all Christian doctrines " as impious, ridiculous and contradictory to the justice of God and the reason of man. . . ." In conclusion, the author called upon " the religious and moral deist " to assert his faith, since deism could not be considered as disgraceful to a virtuous man's character. This article was hotly resented by the faithful and was answered by Aaron Dexter, Professor of Chemistry and Materia Medica at Harvard, under the pseudonym of a " Rational Christian ".

About this time, " a religious and moral deist " proclaimed his faith in no uncertain terms. Convinced that the clergy had subverted the " religion of Reason, Nature and Truth ", Ethan Allen published a distinctly anti-Christian work,

Reason the Only Oracle of Man. During his youth, the future leader of the Green Mountain " boys " came into contact with an English physician, Thomas Young, who probably acquainted him with Blount and other deistic writers. It is believed that Allen and Young at first agreed to write a freethinking work together but later decided that the one who outlived the other was to publish the book. Since Allen survived Young, he inherited the latter's notes.[17] In his preface to *Reason, the Only Oracle of Man,* Allen frankly admitted that he was not a Christian and consequently his book was one long diatribe against the religion of his birth. In condemning the Trinitarian doctrine as unreasonable and unintelligible, and in discarding a belief in the original fall of man as irrational and " chimerical ",[18] he repudiated the basic tenets of the Christian creed. Furthermore, he rejected prophecies on the ground that they were often vague, questionable and contradictory. Likewise he discarded miracles since their performance implied that God had created an imperfect machine.[19] Pointing out the possibilities of Biblical fallibility, Allen rejected the divine origin of the Scriptures and assailed particularly the Old Testament accounts of the creation of the world and the death of Moses.[20] Anticipating Paine, the hero of Ticonderoga showed how impossible it was for Moses to have written that portion of Deuteronomy which dealt with an account of his

[17] J. Pell, *Ethan Allen* (Boston, 1929), pp. 16, 226; H. Hall, *Ethan Allen, the Robin Hood of Vermont* (New York, 1892), p. 21; and Koch, *Republican Religion*, pp. 31-2.

[18] Allen, *Reason, the Only Oracle of Man* (New York, 1836), pp. 73, 81-2. In view of his Trinitarian position, Allen rejected the divinity of Jesus (pp. 75-6).

[19] Concerning the arguments against prophecies see *ibid.*, pp. 52-7, 62-6; and those against miracles, pp. 40-6.

[20] *Ibid.*, pp. 13-4, 42, 59.

own death.[21]   In short, the work was a rejection of revealed religion in general, and Christianity in particular.

Allen's repudiation of Christianity was based on his conviction of the sufficiency of natural religion.   To him, reason, upon which true religion must be based, would lead men to exalt God and to practice morality.   Like his fellow-deists, he accepted the existence of one God and the human duty of divine worship.   Virtuous living, which conformed to "right reason", was conducive to happiness and those practicing it would be rewarded here and hereafter.[22]   Since the religion of nature was rational, it was "universally promulgated to mankind. . . ."   In brief, Ethan Allen attempted from a positive viewpoint to substitute for the particular revelation of the Christian faith the all-embracing revelation of natural religion.

Although *Reason, the Only Oracle of Man* was later described by one sympathetic observer as "a work valuable from its own intrinsic merits . . .", it was far from being either original or intellectually stimulating.   Yet, because it was among the first anti-Christian works to be produced in America, its author attracted some attention.   The poetic Dwight of Yale described Allen in the following lines:

> In vain thro realms of nonsense . . . . . ran
> The great clodhopping oracle of man.
> Yet faithful were his toils: What could he more?
> In Satan's cause he bustled, bruised and swore.

Another staunch defender of the faith pictured Allen as " an ignorant and profane deist . . . who died with a mind replete with horror and despair. . . ."   Still a third believer, not content to have him die in this manner, con-

---

[21] Compare Allen, *ibid.*, p. 59 with Paine, *Age of Reason*, pt. ii, p. 107.
[22] *Ibid.*, pp. 7-9, 20, 29, 97, 100.

signed him to the punishments of the infernal regions. In
his diary, Ezra Stiles, President of Yale College, wrote that
on February 13, 1789 there " died in Vermont the profane
and impious Deist Gen. Ethan Allen, Author of the ' Oracle
of Reason', a book replete with scurrillous Reflexions on
Revelation. . . ." The good clergyman piously added
" ' And in Hell he lift up his Eyes being in Torments.' " [23]

Because of a fire in the printer's garret almost all of the
copies of Allen's work were destroyed. Yet, the few which
remained circulated rather widely. William Bentley, a liberal clergyman of Salem, loaned the book to a Colonel C.
who promised to keep the transaction a secret. He, in turn,
loaned the work to a Mr. Grafton who soon died a " Confirmed Infidel." The relatives of the latter found the book
in the dead man's home. Since the treatise was initialed
W. B. (William Bentley), Bentley was accused of being its
owner and of encouraging skepticism.[24] Another evidence
of the circulation of *Reason, the Only Oracle of Man* was an
article appearing in *The Country Journal and the Poughkeepsie Advertiser* for September 12, 1787 (no. 110). The
writer, describing himself as " Black Beard ", compared
Rhode Island with the Barbary States. He thought that the
principles of these two commonwealths were similar in every
respect " except in religion, and in this they may become
nearly so by . . . adopting the ' Oracle of Reason ' for an
Alcoran. . . ."

Another Revolutionary War leader, Charles Lee, was
accused of being " an enemy of religion ". In a letter to

---

[23] E. Stiles, *Diary*, ed. Dexter, vol. iii, p. 345; U. Ogden, *Antidote to
Deism* (Newark, 1795), vol. ii, p. 270 (footnote) ; T. Dwight, *Triumph
of Infidelity* (New York, 1788), pp. 23-4; *Travels in New England and
New York* (London, 1823), vol. ii, pp. 387-8; and the *Free Enquirer*,
April 8, 1829, vol. i, p. 191.

[24] W. Bentley, *Diary*, November, 1787, vol. i, p. 82.

Dr. Benjamin Rush, dated September 26, 1779, Lee denied the charge and, in the characteristic fashion of an eighteenth-century deist, he pointed out that " no Society [could] exist without religion "; that of all faiths " the most excellent " was that of Christianity provided it was " unincumbered of its sophistications ".   On another occasion, he informed the celebrated Philadelphian physician of his desire to become an orthodox Christian.   With this in mind, he read Dr. Warburton's account of the divine laws of Moses but, as he put it, his choice was " injudicious " for he went away utterly detesting " the God of the Jews."   He consequently asked Dr. Rush to " recommend [him] to some other Apothecary. . . ." [25]   In his will, Lee showed his deistic inclinations; he gave his soul to

the Creator of all worlds and of all creatures; who must from his visible attributes, be indifferent to their modes of worship or creeds, whether Christians, Mahometans or Jews; whether instilled by education, or taken up by reflection; whether more or less absurd; as a weak mortal can no more be answerable for his persuasions, notions, or even skepticism in religion, than for the colour of his skin.[26]

Regarded as " erratic and untrustworthy ", General Lee was at least logical in his refusal to be buried in a church or churchyard on the ground that he did not choose to continue to keep " bad company " when dead.[27]   Less outspoken than Lee, Willie Jones of North Carolina, merchant, planter and member of the Continental Congress, was a freethinker on the style of Jefferson.   Like the Virginian, he hated the

[25] *The Lee Papers*, vol. iii, p. 468 (New York Historical Society *Collections*, 1871-74).

[26] *Ibid.*, vol. iv, pp. 31-2.

[27] *Ibid.*, vol. iv, p. 31. See also Meade, *Old Churches, etc.*, vol. ii, p. 308 and Fiske, *Essays Historical and Literary* (New York, 1902), vol. i, p. 64.

clergy and consequently directed his heirs not to allow any minister to say anything over his body.   Still another prominent Revolutionary figure, Stephen Hopkins, Governor of Rhode Island, was a freethinker or, at least, was so regarded by his contemporaries.   Under the date of July 20, 1785, Ezra Stiles, in commenting on the death of the former governor, wrote that he was convinced that the friends of Hopkins were correct in describing him as a deist.   The good President of Yale continued: " He was a Man of a Noble fortitude & Resolution.   He was a glorious Patriot!—[but Jesus will say unto him *I know you not*]."

In the meantime, a Boston magazine was reproducing the writings of leading European deists.   Voltaire's prayer addressed to the " God of all beings, of all worlds and of all ages . . ." was republished from his *Treatise on Toleration*.[28] Another deistic composition appeared in a New York periodical, *The American Magazine*.   In 1788, its readers were requested by " Candidus " to explain certain supposed discrepancies in the New Testament accounts as to the genealogy of Jesus, his anointing by a woman, his being reviled on the cross by thieves and the actual hour of his crucifixion.   The writer ironically stated that any gentleman who reconciled the different accounts of the Evangelists " would deserve the thanks of his christian friends."   He was answered in the very next number by another anonymous writer who not only attempted to resolve his deistic opponent's doubts but also advised " Candidus " to read a few books on the evidences of Christianity.[29]   In addition to the magazines, the newspapers served to spread deistic speculation.   *The Country Journal and Dutchess and Ulster County Farmer's Register* for January 20, 1789 (no. 181) published upon request an article in which some imaginary Indian chiefs advocated

---

[28] *The Boston Magazine*, June, 1784 (no. 8), vol. i, pp. 338-9.

[29] *The American Magazine*, May, 1788, pp. 420-1 ; June, 1788, pp. 491-2.

deistic principles.   This composition was similar to one published in 1752 by James Parker.[30]

As a result of increased activity, especially after 1783, deism began to spread among the people some of whom discussed and openly espoused its cause.   In 1772, Francis Asbury, a Methodist-Episcopalian minister, making a trip from Trenton to Philadelphia, met a group of men whom he described as "stupidly ignorant, sceptical [and] deistical. . . ."   That deism was a common topic of conversation is shown in letters addressed to newspapers.   One correspondent, in the *New-York Packet* for March 24, 1785 (no. 474), informed his readers that he, together with a clergyman and two others, argued the merits of revealed religion.   Another writer, "Pietas", sent a letter to the same newspaper in which he denounced all who aired skeptical thoughts without the least provocation.   In this communication, the correspondent related that upon one occasion he was in the company of a rather elderly gentleman and a number of "young wits".   Without any reason, the young men presented arguments against Christianity whereupon the older man impressed upon them the uselessness of their "profanity."[31]

The constituted authorities were aware of the social and political dynamite frequently hidden in apparently harmless religious or intellectual heresies, and sometimes intervened to check the progress of deism.   John Dickinson, President of the State of Delaware, issued, in 1781, a proclamation against freethinking which was reprinted in *The Pennsylvania Gazette and Weekly Advertiser* for June 23, 1782.   In an introductory article, the editor congratulated Dickinson

[30] See chapter iii, p. 77. It is interesting to note that this same speech was reproduced in a deistic New York newspaper, *The Correspondent*, January 5, 1828 (No. 24), vol. ii, pp. 372-4.

[31] *New-York Packet*, April 28, 1785 (No. 484). This letter was addressed to the *American Spectator*. For Asbury's observation see his *Journal* (New York, 1821), vol. i, p. 120.

upon his advocacy of revealed religion and observed that a pronouncement from so distinguished a personage would do much to check " vice and infidelity ".   The Delaware proclamation called upon all rational creatures to submit to the holy laws of God, to attend His worship and to practice true virtue.   Moreover, it called upon the magistrates to prosecute and punish all who were guilty of blasphemy or profanity. Dickinson's proclamation was followed by a number of newspaper and magazine articles written by pious Christians to stem the deistic tide.   The young were especially warned against the pitfalls of deistic speculation.   In *The Providence Gazette and Country Journal* for September 24, 1785 (no. 1134), the work of a noted English Dissenter, Dr. Isaac Watts (1674-1748), on *Advice To a Young Man, upon His Entrance into the World,* was reprinted.   The famous hymn writer counselled his readers against gambling their "eternal interests in the world to come, upon the mere light of nature. . . ."   Moreover, all those who rejected "the blessings of divine revelation and grace" were conceited and thoughtless.   In the same vein, a Boston newspaper, *The Continental Journal and Weekly Advertiser* for January 5, 1786 (no. 515), warned the people that "the cool and deliberate villainy of infidels [could not] be compared with one hour of conscious rectitude, far less than with their felicity, who at their last moments, have witnessed in what peace a Christian [could] die."

The vagueness of the deistic philosophy was further pointed out by William Livingston, Governor of New Jersey, whose article, "Thoughts on Deism," was printed repeatedly in the magazines of the period under the pseudonym of "Hortensius".[32]   In this essay, the writer asserted that

[32] *The New-Haven Gazette, and the Connecticut Magazine,* June 22, 1786; *The American Museum,* November, 1788 and *The Massachusetts Magazine,* January, 1789. For an eulogistic sermon upon Livingston see the *Universal Asylum,* January, 1791, pp. 7-8.

deists were " superficial reasoners " who preached a morality which did not surpass in practice that exercised by a horse. The light of nature, he held, was an insufficient guide in matters concerning salvation. Could any one, he asked, believe that the moral precepts of Christianity had been destroyed by "the unphilosophical philosophy of a Bolingbroke, or the wretched pun or threadbare jest of a Voltaire or a Rousseau "? Deism, unlike Christianity, could not account for the entrance of sin into the world, or could not prove the immortality of the soul. In conclusion, " Hortensius " represented the deists as simple blockheads.

Deism was answered not only with ridicule but also with a reasoned defense of Christian miracles and prophecies. Upon these evidences the validity of the Biblical revelation was believed to rest; consequently the faithful were extremely anxious to popularize their views. In 1785, in a series of newspaper articles, "American Spectator " defended the necessity of a " particular Providence " and the truth of Christianity. In order to vindicate his first position, he held that it would be absurd to imagine that the Deity created worlds only to forget them. From this, he concluded that a miracle-working Providence existed. That Christianity was of divine origin could be attested by its prophecies, miracles, moral excellence, and rapid spread.[33] Similarly, a writer in a New Haven periodical sought to prove the truth of the Christian revelation. To him, miracles were not only possible, since the Deity could suspend or alter natural laws, but also rational since they were as much an evidence of divine power as His natural works. Especially did he defend the miracles of Jesus as both divine and duly attested. Furthermore, he doubted whether the deists would have believed the miracles of Jesus, even if they had actually wit-

[33] *New-York Packet*, August 29, September 19, October 3 and 10, 1785 (Nos. 519, 525, 529, 531).

nessed their performance.[34] A New Jersey magazine also
came to the aid of Christian evidences. The very aim of
The Christian's, Scholar's and Farmer's Magazine was " to
advance the general interests of our holy religion. . . ."
That Jesus actually lived, that he was the Messiah and that
the morality of the New Testament was consistent with divine
goodness were argued by the orthodox within the pages of
this Elizabethtown magazine.[35]

The champions of Christianity attacked deistic speculation
through the medium not only of periodicals but also of
lectures. In 1783, William Hazlitt, an English Unitarian,
came to America and, during that year and the one following,
delivered a series of public discourses in Philadelphia and
Boston. His talks were well attended and favorably
received. In one sermon, he associated American prosperity
with belief in the Christian revelation and pleaded with his
hearers to teach the Scriptures to their children and servants.
He urged, however, the encouragement of free enquiry in
the hope that by such a procedure Christianity would be
purged of its accretions.[36] From a more orthodox stand-
point, Ezra Stiles delivered sermons designed to support the
Christian revelation. In an Election Day address (1783),
he assailed the arguments of Hume, Voltaire, Tindal and
that " amiable Confucius of Deism," Shaftesbury. He also
condemned the deistic procedure of glorifying all religions
but that of Christianity. Stiles took the position that deism
could not be checked " by hiding the Deistical writings "
but by refuting them and consequently, as President of Yale,

[34] *The New-Haven Gazette* and *Connecticut Magazine*, November 30,
December 7, 14 and 21, 1786 (Nos. 42-45). These essays were entitled
"A Dissertation on Miracles".

[35] *The Christian's, Scholar's, and Farmer's Magazine*, vol. i, pp. 18-22,
149, 153, 286, 408-11.

[36] W. Hazlitt, *A Thanksgiving Discourse*, December 15, 1785 (Boston,
1786), pp. 8-11, 13-17.

he allowed his students to debate such subjects as whether the historical parts of the Bible were of divine inspiration; whether there was anything in the Scriptures which was contradictory to reason; and whether religion had on the whole benefited mankind.   In 1790, the good minister requested the aged Franklin to state his religious views, especially those concerning Jesus of Nazareth.   In his answer, the venerable Doctor affirmed his faith in the deistic creed of his youth. Subscribing to the three basic tenets of natural religion, he refused to say a single word as to the need of supplementing these articles by any revealed religion.   In regard to Jesus, Franklin was convinced that his original system of morality and religion, before it became corrupted, was " the best the World ever saw or is likely to see. . . ."   The skeptical philosopher, however, had some doubts as to the divinity of Christ.   Tactful to the end, the eighty-four year old man thought that it was needless for him to busy himself with the question because he soon expected to have "an Opportunity to know the Truth with less Trouble. . . ." [87]

As the Revolutionary era was drawing to a close, the northern defenders of orthodoxy secured an addition to their ranks in the person of Timothy Dwight whose *Triumph of Infidelity* appeared in 1788.   In the opinion of Stiles, Dwight's poetic work harmed rather than promoted the cause he intended to defend, since the author had not confined himself to a criticism of the deists, but had gone so far as to vilify them with an acrimony decidedly un-Christian. [88]   *The Triumph of Infidelity* was addressed to Voltaire, who had taught that " the chief end of man was to slander his God, and abuse him forever."   In the poem proper, such English deists as Herbert and Bolingbroke were described as leaders

[87] Stiles, *Diary*, ed. Dexter, vol. iii, p. 387; Franklin, *Writings*, ed. Smyth, vol. x, p. 84.

[88] E. Stiles, *Diary*, ed. Dexter, vol. iii, p. 326 (August 15, 1788).

in " Satan's cause ". Moreover, these thinkers had been aided in their iniquity by such lesser lights as Toland, Tindal, Collins, Chubb, Morgan and Woolston, all of whom "help'd rakes to sin. . . ." [39] If these deists were to win the day, usury and immorality would be widespread, since modern freethinkers were free from all principles and virtues. Roundly abusing the " heathen " ideas of the Chinese, Dwight indirectly assailed those deists who were accustomed to praise all faiths except that of Christianity. In a hopeful note, the satire ended with the prophecy that virtue would triumph over vice, true religion over " infidelity ".

The poem was rather harshly criticized in the July 1788 number of *The American Magazine.* Its editor, Noah Webster, who reviewed the work, was at that time on unfriendly terms with Dwight because the latter had just agreed to contribute to *The American Museum,* a rival periodical published by Carey. While Webster was willing to admit that *The Triumph of Infidelity* had some poetic merit, he felt that it could never pass for true wit or good satire. He severely censured Dwight for his abusive description of the religious ideas of the Chinese. This the critic thought had been written because the Chinese were not Christians. Webster further held that Dwight was a "theological dogmatist" who was not destined to achieve a heaven reserved for love and benevolence. This article, however, was not typical of the religious ideas of Noah Webster which were distinctly orthodox. The celebrated lexicographer was brought up in a Calvinistic household and although, according to his own testimony, he at first became a " rational Christian ", he later defended evangelicalism. He even went so far as to contribute to the *Panoplist,* an orthodox magazine of the early nineteenth century, and one of his articles was printed in

---

[39] Dwight, *Triumph of Infidelity,* p. 16. As for Voltaire, Dwight thought him so superficial a reasoner that he could prove anything (p. 18).

pamphlet form under the title of *The Peculiar Doctrines of the Gospel Explained and Defended*.   In this work, he defended the Calvinistic doctrines of predestination and election, affirmed his belief in the historic truthfulness of the Bible and accepted the miracles of Jesus as evidences of his divine mission.   In conclusion, Webster regretted to see " a large portion of the world so inattentive to religion." [40]

As during the provincial period, so now, deistic speculation was less conspicious in the South than in the North.   Yet, in Virginia, it was more prevalent than ever before, chiefly because of an increasing anti-clerical spirit stimulated, in turn, by the struggle for the disestablishment of the Anglican Church.   Up to 1776, the fight waged in Virginia by the dissenting denominations was one for religious toleration; after that year, it became a battle for religious liberty.   In 1776, a law was passed suspending the salaries of Anglican clergymen with the result that many of them were forced to leave their flocks.   Eight years later, the Dissenters won a notable victory by defeating the general assessment bill providing for the support of religious teachers.   Though in the same year, the Episcopalians recovered some lost ground through the passage of an incorporation act, their victory was shortlived and the following year brought the passage of the Act for Establishing Religious Freedom.

The Presbyterians and Baptists of Virginia were aided in their struggle to disestablish the Anglican Church by the deistic Jefferson and the liberal Madison.   Both of these men, moved by an anti-clerical spirit, objected to grants of public funds for religious support.   They were opposed by Patrick Henry whose hostility to deism made him associate that movement with everything vicious and depraved.   The

[40] Scudder, *Noah Webster* (Boston, 1882), pp. 167-8; and Noah Webster, *The Peculiar Doctrines of the Gospel Explained and Defended* (Poughkeepsie, 1809), pp. 8-9, 13, 15.

fight for disestablishment naturally stimulated an interest in religious questions and made the more advanced thinkers react with such force against Christianity that they were drawn into the deistic camp. Ruring the Revolutionary era a large number of prominent Virginian statesmen were either deists at one time or another or held liberal religious views. Coming under the last category were such notable figures as Washington, Mason and Madison. Washington, because of his great popularity, was and still is claimed alike by the friends of orthodoxy and of freethinking. As early as 1800, Jefferson remarked that, according to Gouverneur Morris, the Father of his Country did not subscribe to the Christian system of religion. Thirty years later, another freethinker, Frances Wright, declared in a speech that " . . . Washington was not a Christian—that is, he believed not in the priest's God, nor in the divine authority of the priest's book." [41] Since then, others have classified him as a deist.[42] The stand taken by this group has been based on the evidence that Washington always mentioned God in deistic rather than Biblical phraseology, that he refused to kneel in prayer or request the presence of a clergyman at his death-bed and that he continually refrained from making any affirmative statement in support of Christianity. In answer to these contentions, the orthodox have presented such counter-proofs as the testimony of his contemporaries, the " high religious motives " actuating his military leadership, his attendance at church and service as vestryman, his reference in 1783 to the " benign influence " of revelation, his response to religious

[41] T. Jefferson, *Writings*, ed. P. L. Ford (New York, 1892), vol. i, p. 284; Wright, *Course of Popular Lectures* (New York, 1831), pp. 10-11.

[42] J. McCabe, " Six Infidel Presidents " (*Haldeman-Julius Quarterly* April, 1927, pp. 37-40) ; J. M. Robertson, *Short History of Free Thought* (London, 1915), vol. ii, pp. 382-3; W. E. Woodward, *George Washington* (New York, 1926), p. 284; and R. Hughes, *George Washington, 1777-1781* (New York, 1930), pp. 270-98 (especially pp. 286-98).

denominations in 1789, and his farewell address.[43] With
such conflicting assertions based equally on well established
facts and utterances, the classification of Washington in a
definite category is impossible. To one not interested in
furthering causes it is apparent that the Virginian professed
to be a Christian, although he showed the deistic tendencies
of his age. His skeptical leanings, however, were never
strong enough to make him openly renounce Christianity.
If anything, he should have desired it to continue as a vital
force in the life of the young Republic because he was firmly
convinced that religion and morality were " the essentials
pillars of civil society. . . ."

George Mason was even less deistic in tendency than Washington. Although regarded as a liberal in religion, he was
never accused by his contemporaries of being a freethinker
or deist. He was a regular church member, a vestryman and
together with Washington supervised the construction of a
house of worship. Mason believed firmly in the doctrine
of religious liberty and true to his convictions he took an
active part in the disestablishment of the Anglican Church in
Virginia. His course throughout the struggle was a consistent one; as a liberal, he desired to see the Anglican Church
placed on an equal footing with others; as a Christian, he
wanted the church to continue its functions and therefore
fought to secure its property. His liberal religious views
were reflected in the Virginia Bill of Rights and although
some claim that Henry was the author of its religious clauses,
it appears that Mason composed them.[44] To Mason, religion

[43] W. Meade, *Old Churches, etc.*, vol. ii, pp. 243-5; G. Washington,
Writings, ed. J. Sparks (Boston, 1855), vol. xii, pp. 399-403, 411 (Reli-
gious Opinions and Habits of Washington); George Washington, *The
Christian* (issued by U. S. George Washington Bicentennial Commission,
prepared by A. B. Hart), (Washington, 1931), pp. 1-16; and Sears,
George Washington (New York, 1932), pp. 6-7, 113, 127-8, 254, 322, 409.

[44] The religious provisions of the Virginia Bill of Rights have been

was simply the duty owed by man to his Creator. It was to be discharged by the individual as his reason and conviction dictated. In the exercise of religion, man was to enjoy the fullest toleration. Mason believed that it was " the mutual duty of all to practice Christian forbearance, love and charity towards each other." [45]

Like other Virginians, James Madison, historical, legal and theological scholar, was caught up by the deistic currents of his age and was almost swept into the deistic whirlpool. As an ardent advocate of religious liberty, he viewed with disgust the " diabolical, hell-conceived principles of persecution " which prevailed among Christian sects and to which " business " the clergy were always eager to furnish " their " quota of imps. . . ." During the struggle for disestablishment, Madison made an important speech on the question of the Assessment Bill. Desiring to know upon what basis the courts would decide what constituted Christianity, the future President was led to raise such skeptical questions as : Was the entire Bible or only a few of its parts inspired? What copy, translation or edition of the Scriptures would be used? Unfortunately, Madison did not answer the questions which he raised and therefore the extent of his deistic leanings remains problematic. At least, this seems

ascribed to Henry on the basis of Edmund Randolph's testimony written thirty years after the events took place. Randolph's statement is unsupported by contemporary evidence; nowhere did Henry assert his authorship of these articles nor was such a claim made during his lifetime. Conway, the biographer of Edmund Randolph, thinks that Randolph was mistaken in the entire matter. (M. D. Conway, *Omitted Chapters of History Disclosed in the Life and Papers of Edmund Randolph* [New York, 1889], p. 158). On the other hand, Mason himself declared that he wrote the Bill of Rights. (Rowland, *The Life of George Mason* [New York, 1892], vol. i, pp. 236-8).

[45] J. Madison, *Writings*, ed. Hunt (New York, 1900), vol. i, p. 40; Rowland, *op. cit.*, vol. i, pp. 84, 113, 241, 243-4, 344; and Sherlock, *Tall Timbers* (Boston, 1926), pp. 12-3, 33.

certain: the Virginian never rejected Christianity; on the
contrary in a letter written as late as 1832, he described it
as " the best and purest religion." [46]

More to the left than Madison, Mason or Washington was
Thomas Jefferson, whose position was typical of the American climate of deistic opinion, which desired the reformation
and not destruction of Christianity.   Convinced that the
" real " enemies of the gentle Jesus were the clergy, he proposed to strip them of their power.   To accomplish this end,
the Sage of Monticello adopted a rather cautious approach;
instead of aggressively assailing the Biblical revelation upon
which priestly authority rested, he contented himself with
drawing a nice distinction between " the religion of the
priests and that of the Gospels."   The first he desired to
overthrow; the second, which he considered to be natural
religion, he wished to restore.   Interested in the intellectual
concerns of the age, the prominent Virginian read Bolingbroke, Shaftesbury, Priestley, Voltaire and Rousseau.[47]   In
spite of his acquaintance with the writings of Voltaire,
Jefferson's deism was not that of the militant French school;
rather was it similar to the position of such English deists as
Tindal and Chubb who were anxious " to save " Christianity.
To the author of the American Declaration of Independence,
reason was to be given first place in the task of reforming

[46] Madison, *Writings*, ed. Hunt, vol. i, p. 21, vol. ii, pp. 88-9, vol. ix,
p. 485; Meade, *Old Churches, etc.*, vol. ii, pp. 99-100; and Rives, *Life and
Times of James Madison* (Boston, 1859), vol. i, p. 603.

[47] Jefferson, *Writings*, ed. Ford (New York, 1892), vol. ii, p. 95;
Chinard, *Thomas Jefferson* (Boston, 1929), p. 26; B. Faÿ, *Revolutionary
Spirit in France and America* (New York, 1928), p. 78; H. S. Randall,
Life of Thomas Jefferson (New York, 1858), p. 556 and Riley, *American
Philosophy* (New York, 1907), pp. 268-9.   Both Riley and Randall con-
tend that Priestley, the English Unitarian, exerted a tremendous influence
upon Jefferson's religious views.   According to Chinard, Jefferson owed
very little to Bolingbroke but a great deal to the Stoic philosophers of
Greece with whose ideas he came in contact through Cicero.

the Christian religion which was to be purged of its existing corruptions. To Jefferson, the moral system of Jesus was " the most benevolent and sublime probably that has ever been taught. . . ." The moral precepts of Christ, however, had been corrupted by those pretending to be his disciples. In reality, these false prophets had

disfigured and sophisticated his actions and precepts, from views of personal interest, so as to induce the unthinking part of mankind to throw off the whole system in disgust, and to pass sentence as an impostor on the most innocent, the most benevolent, the most eloquent and sublime character that has ever been exhibited to man. . . .[48]

The Sage of Monticello endeavored to recall Christians to the simple gospel first expounded by Christ. This gospel was in reality a restatement of the religion of nature, since it taught a belief in one God, the practice of virtue and the existence of a future state.[49] For his deistic leanings, Jefferson was bitterly assailed by the New England clergy. Although described in 1784 by the Reverend Dr. Stiles as " a truly scientific and learned Man—and every way excellent . . .", by 1800 he was characterized by the Congregational ministry as "the arch-apostle of the cause of irreligion and freethought." [50] This change in tone was undoubtedly due as much to Jefferson's political as to his religious views.

Unlike the third American President, neither Edmund nor John Randolph remained true to the deistic faith of their youth. While a student at William and Mary, Edmund Randolph was " poisoned " by two of his " preceptors, who,

[48] Jefferson, *Writings*, ed. Ford, vol. viii, p. 225.

[49] *Ibid.*, vol. iii, p. 264; vol. iv, pp. 430, 432; vol. viii, pp. 21-2, 224-5 (footnote), 228.

[50] Stiles, *Diary*, ed. Dexter, vol. iii, p. 125; Stauffer, *New England and the Bavarian Illuminati* (New York, 1918), p. 121.

though of the ministry," encouraged him to read books on
" infidelity ".   In a like fashion, Thomas Jefferson was probably open to the same " pernicious " influences during his
student days at the Williamsburg seat of learning.   Here, in
the early 'sixties, he came in contact with a liberal-minded
professor, William Small, and a deistically-inclined future
professor, George Wythe, both of whom exerted an influence
upon the impressionable young man.   "Infidelity" at
William and Mary was, however, fought by the forces of
orthodoxy which opposed the appointment of any trustee
who was not a Christian.   In fact, John Randolph (1728-
1784), the father of Edmund, was twice rejected as a Visitor
of William and Mary College because he was regarded as a
deist.   Edmund Randolph followed in his father's footsteps;
according to his own testimony given many years later, he
was so confirmed a deist in 1776 that had it not been for
the piety of his wife he might never have forsaken his
" infidel " views.   Her " sacred regard " for the Bible eventually " converted " him to Christianity; in the last years of
his life he found comfort in Wesley's sermons.[51]   Another
Randolph, John of Roanoke, strayed from the fold and
became a champion of an unpopular cause.   Influenced by
Shaftesbury, Bolingbroke, Gibbon, Voltaire and Rousseau,[52]

[51] Conway, *Omitted Chapters of History Disclosed in the Life and
Papers of Edmund Randolph*, pp. 12, 156, 389, 391 and Meade, *Old
Churches, etc.*, vol. i, p. 182 and vol. ii, pp. 292-3.

[52] Garland, *Life of John Randolph of Roanoke* (New York, 1851), vol.
ii, p. 652, H. M. Jones, *America and French Culture* (Durham, 1927),
p. 367. One of the first books which Randolph read was Voltaire's
Charles XII (Letters of John Randolph to a Young Relative [Phila-
delphia, 1834], p. 190). In fact, his library contained some seventy
volumes of the works of this French cynic. In addition to Voltaire, the
deistic works of Gibbon and Rousseau together with the atheistic tracts
of Hume and Diderot were included in his library collection. (Garland,
ibid., vol. ii, pp. 9-10 and *Letters of John Randolph to a Young Relative*,
p. 41).

he condemned Christianity as vigorously as did Ethan Allen but, unlike the latter, he generally did not take the trouble of putting his deistic thoughts on paper. On one occasion, however, he did so, as his notes approving the position of Gibbon indicate. Although he later repudiated these as " horrible " examples of sophisms, they nevertheless reflected the deistic inclinations of his youth. It was not until 1817 that he made his peace with Christianity. In a letter to Francis Scott Key, composer of the Star-Spangled Banner, he announced in that year that he was reconciled to his God and was assured of His pardon through faith in Christ.[53]

[53] Garland, *ibid.*, vol. ii, pp. 66-9, 97-100, 102, 652-3; Meade, *Old Churches, etc.*, vol. ii, p. 459 (Appendix, No. X) and H. Adams, *John Randolph* (New York, 1898), p. 14.

CHAPTER V

Deism Militant: Early National Period (1789-1805)

From 1789 to 1805, deism assailed more vigorously than ever before the supernatural revelation of Christianity. Paine, Volney and Palmer, though not typical of the American movement, were nevertheless examples of its rising militancy. By means of popularized accounts, they spread the notion that traditional Christianity would disappear before deism as inevitably as the morning mist before the rising sun. The deistic tendency was distinguished not only by its greater aggressiveness but also by its greater appeal. Up to the time of Paine, deism was an aristocratic cult confined almost solely to the "well-to-do classes." With the publication of *The Age of Reason,* the axis about which deistic thought in America rotated, the new ideology reached the rural and urban masses. Volney's *Ruins: or a Survey of the Revolutions of Empires* continued the work of Paine, while Palmer, the outstanding American-born deist, established societies, lectureships and newspapers in order to propagate the "new religion".

The tendency toward a greater degree of deistic militancy was occasioned by clerical opposition to the principles of the French Revolution. To save republicanism and equalitarianism from ecclesiastical destruction, the advance guard of liberalism, composed of Paine and Palmer, tried to discredit the clergy by showing that the Biblical revelation upon which clerical authority rested was a human and not a divine document. The attack was led by Paine whose *Age of Reason* was the first blast of deistic dynamite to disturb the complacency of the faithful. So profoundly were they

120

shocked by this work that its author, Thomas Paine, was treated with such deep and relentless hatred that his undeserved reputation of "a filthy little atheist" has survived him by more than a century. He was repeatedly described by his opponents as an inveterate drunkard, a superficial reasoner, a malignant blasphemer and an impious atheist.[1] The vilification of Paine was due to the fact that he was guilty of carrying heresy to the people. The popularity of his early pamphlets and his earnestness in attacking dogmas common to all denominations were considered revolutionary. No longer was deism confined to people of education and social prominence; it was now spread among the masses. It was said that *The Age of Reason* could be found in practically every village in America and that it was tending to "unchristianize" nominal believers. Boys engaged in dressing flax, students enrolled in leading colleges, men enjoying the hospitality of convivial taverns were reading or eagerly discussing Paine's tract. Consequently, according to one account, tens of thousands proceeded to desert their faith, while millions were led to applaud—probably an exaggerated estimate.[2] The extensive circulation of Paine's pamphlet was

[1] J. Adams, *Works*, ed. C. F. Adams, vol. ix, p. 627; Levi, *Defence of the Old Testament* (New York, 1797), p. 5; Nelson, *An Investigation of that False, Fabulous, etc.* (Lancaster, 1800), pp. 10-11, 41, 45; Ogden, *Antidote to Deism*, vol. i, pp. 15, 18, 122, vol. ii, p. 297; Gouverneur Morris, *Writings*, ed. Sparks (Boston, 1832), vol. ii, p. 409, vol. iii, p. 46; and Watson, *Apology for the Bible* (Albany, 1796), pp. 3-4. Also consult Conway, *Life of Thomas Paine* (New York, 1892), vol. ii, pp. 181-190. For the characterization quoted above see T. Roosevelt, *Gouverneur Morris* (Boston, 1891), p. 289.

[2] D. Nelson, *Cause and Cure for Infidelity* (New York, 1841), p. 258. Consult also *Theological Magazine*, March, April and May, 1798, vol. iii, p. 187; Priestly, *Observations on the Increase of Infidelity* (Philadelphia, 1797), p. 53; Beecher, *Autobiography*, ed. C. Beecher (New York, 1864), vol. i, pp. 48-9; Francis, *New York during the last Half a Century* (New York, 1857), p. 89 and the Massachusetts Historical Society *Collections*, vol. iv, 6th series (Boston, 1891), pp. 585, 614 (Letters written by Brown to Belknap, February 6 and 25, 1797).

due to the fact that it was brought to the attention of people through newspaper advertisements [3] and orthodox replies; [4] that it was distributed free of charge by deistic organizations; [5] and that it was written in a style likely to be understood by the average man.

If left to himself, Paine might have continued indefinitely his life-long resolution of not wishing to discredit openly the Christian religion; circumstances, however, intervened.[6] During the French Revolution, most of the higher clergy of the Catholic Church allied themselves with the monarchy and thus were associated with the forces of reaction. In order to overthrow the alliance of throne and altar and thereby save republican and equilitarian principles, Paine determined to destroy the priesthood by putting an end to the source of their authority—the Biblical revelation. The growth of atheism, which was endangering the existence of the only true religion—deism, was another consideration motivating the Anglo-American to attack the divine origin of the Scriptures. To him, disbelief in God and a future state was occasioned by the disgust men felt for the fanatical and reactionary tendencies of the clergy. To save deism and republicanism, Paine published the first part of his *Age of Reason* (1794). This was devoted to a generalized attack upon revealed religion. The author argued that the word of God was not to be found in any written or spoken expression but in the Creation itself. Moreover, the Biblical account was not

[3] Thomas' *Massachusetts Spy or the Worcester Gazette*, November 19, 1794 (no. 1128), August 13, 1796 (no. 1220), September 7, 1796 (no. 1221); *The American Mercury*, July 21, 1794 (vol. ix, no. 524) and *The Mercury*, October 28-31, 1794 (no. 216).

[4] For these replies see chapter vi, pp. 164-7.

[5] Riley, *American Philosophy*, p. 305 and Ruttenber, *History of the Town of Newburgh* (Newburgh, 1859), pp. 87-8.

[6] H. H. Clark, *Toward a Reinterpretation of Thomas Paine* (in American Literature, vol. v, no. 2, May, 1933, pp. 135-6).

binding upon future generations because it could not be regarded as a revelation, which, according to Paine, was a direct message communicated by God to man. Its stories of miracles and prophecies were false because the former were invented by impostors and were derogatory to the Deity and nature and because the latter were vague and indefinite. These "evidences", having been added to "fabulous religion", were not necessary to true faith.[7] The genuine creed consisted in a belief in the existence of one God and the practice of virtue. Although not greatly concerned with the problem of immortality, Paine accepted the idea of a future state.

Whereas the first part of *The Age of Reason* dealt with revelation in general, the second discussed the Judaic-Christian account in particular. One by one, Paine submitted the books of the Old Testament to the dictates of reason—only to find them wanting. Asserting that their authenticity depended upon the certainty of their authorship and upon the credit to be given to their testimony, he attempted to prove that Moses, Joshua, Samuel, David and Solomon did not compose the books bearing their names. In fact, the Pentateuch was written "by some very ignorant and stupid pretenders to authorship, several hundred years after the death of Moses. . . ."[8] Moreover, the Hebrew prophets were unimportant figures in their day and Isaiah, who was reputed to have predicted the coming of Jesus, was actually an impostor. Paine held also that the Gospels were not written by the apostles and that they appeared centuries after the death of Christ. He admitted the greatness of Jesus as a

[7] Paine, *Age of Reason* (New York, no date), pp. 8, 21-2, 38, 40, 82, 84-7, 89-90.

[8] For a discussion of the books of Moses consult *ibid.*, pp. 105-20; for those of Joshua, pp. 124-9; for Samuel, p. 134; for the Psalms of David, pp. 155-6 and the Proverbs of Solomon, pp. 156-7.

man but denied that Jesus was God. The life of Christ
was a " fable . . . blasphemously obscene ", his ancestry a
piece of fiction, his immaculate conception an impossible im-
posture and his resurrection doubtful.[9]   Consequently, Paine
repudiated the divine origin of Christianity on the ground
that it was too " absurd for belief, too impossible to convince
and too inconsistent for practice. . . ."   Furthermore, the
Christian religion was " an engine of power " serving the
purpose of despotism as well as " a species of Atheism "
denying God by introducing the necessity of a Redeemer.[10]
Therefore, Paine suggested the introduction of deism which
was unfavorable to tyranny and avarice and which taught
all that was necessary.[11]   A deistic David had arisen to slay
the Goliath of Christendom.

Satisfied that his *Age of Reason* had intellectually disposed
of one enemy to natural religion, Paine turned to its second
foe, atheism.   In 1797, in an address before the Paris
Society of Theophilanthropists, an organization denying the
divine origin of the Bible but accepting the existence of God
and a future state, he assailed the atheistic concept of a
universe which came into being without the aid of an efficient
Agent.   Since the cosmos consisted of matter which did not
possess the property of motion, the rotation of the planets
would be impossible without the assistance of an external
Cause.   Paine held that the prevalence of atheism was due to
the introduction of orthodox religion which created atheists
by its persecutions.   The days of persecution over, atheism
would disappear.[12]   This speech was circulated in America

[9] *Ibid.*, pp. 194, 196-8, 200, 213-5.

[10] *Ibid.*, pp. 248-9. See also pp. 33, 45, 57.

[11] *Ibid.*, pp. 247, 249. For a definition of Deism see p. 216 and for
other references consult pp. 66, 92.

[12] Paine, *A Letter to the Honorable Thomas Erskine . . . with his
Discourse to the Society of the Theophilanthropists* (Paris, 1797), pp.
28-31.

and was reprinted in *The Temple of Reason* for January 3, 1801.

When, in 1802, Paine returned to the United States upon the request of Jefferson, deistic newspapers hailed his arrival, while conservative sheets bitterly lamented it.[13]   In the same year, Samuel Adams sent a letter to the visitor urging him to publish no further work on " infidelity ".   In his answer, Paine cleverly pointed out that if " infidelity " consisted in accepting the existence of God. he was an " infidel." [14]   If Adams had written in the hope of dissuading the champion of natural religion from writing deistic tracts during his American residence, he was destined to disappointment.   In the deistic newspaper, *The Prospect, or View of the Moral World* for February 18, 1804 (no. 11), there appeared an article by Paine which stated that the chief difference between a deist and a Christian was a matter of fact and that fact was the evidence of revelation.   He described Christianity as "the strangest system of religion ever set up " because it committed a murder upon Jesus in order to redeem mankind for the sin of having eaten an apple.[15]

Although the State of New York presented Paine with a farm at New Rochelle, he spent his last years in poverty. Broken in health and reduced in finances, he was forced to move to a miserable lodging house on Fulton Street in New York City.   Just before he died in 1809, two clergymen

[13] Contrast the jubilant article in *The Temple of Reason*, November 6, 1802, vol. ii, p. 287 with several articles published in the *Balance and Columbian Repository*, November 30, December 7 and 14, 1802 (nos. 48-50), vol. i, pp. 377, 385, 393-4.

[14] Paine, *Writings*, ed. Conway (New York, 1894-1896), vol. iv, pp. 201-2, 205.

[15] In subsequent issues a correspondent describing himself as T. P. (probably Thomas Paine) wrote a number of articles attacking Christianity and various Biblical stories.   See the *Prospect or View of the Moral World*, March 3, 10, 24 and April 7, 1804 (nos. 13, 14, 16, 18).

gained access to his room. To their questions concerning his religious opinions, Paine simply said: " Let me alone; good morning." In his will, he mentioned having in manuscript Part III of *The Age of Reason* and also an *Answer to the Bishop of Llandaff*. Only some fragments of these works remain, although, as early as 1802, Paine attempted to find a publisher for them. His friend, Jefferson, however, cautiously " advised and requested him " not to have them printed.[16] Yet, in 1807, most of the work did appear in pamphlet form under the title of *An Examination of the Passages in the New Testament, quoted from the Old and called Prophecies concerning Jesus Christ.*[17] Three years latter, *The Theophilanthropist,* a New York magazine, designed to promote the " mild, tolerant religion of virtue, which the Creator has wisely revealed to the conscience of all mankind . . .", printed Paine's *Answer to Bishop Watson's ' Apology for the Bible '.* In this tract, the deist maintained that the Englishman was wrong in his contention that the Book of Genesis was the oldest work in the world. Paine held that its story of the creation was taken from other peoples and that it was the last book of the Pentateuch to be written. He argued that Job, a Gentile work, was composed before Genesis.[18]

Like Paine's *Age of Reason,* Volney's *Ruins: or a Survey of the Revolutions of Empires* (1791) achieved such popularity that it was spoken of as late as the mid-nineteenth century.[19] Although concerned chiefly with the causes for the

[16] Paine, *Works,* ed. Van der Weyde (New Rochelle, 1925), vol. i, p. 425, Letter from Congressman Eben Elmer to David Moore, December 11, 1802).

[17] This was the last work that Paine ever published. It can be found in Paine, *Works,* ed. Van der Weyde, vol. ix, pp. 205-292.

[18] *The Theophilanthropist,* June (?) and July, 1810 (nos. 6, 7), pp. 220-28, 263-72.

[19] D. Nelson, *Cause and Cure of Infidelity,* p. 238 and R. Owen and A.

fall of ancient empires,[20] the work incidentally touched upon the question of divine revelation. The French savant rejected all supernatural accounts because it was impossible to determine which religion possessed the true evidences. Through the medium of Mohammedan, Indian and Jewish speakers, the former delegate to the French National Assembly ridiculed such Christian doctrines as the divinity of Jesus and original sin. He also derided the gospel precept of turning one's cheek because it degraded the good by making them servile. Furthermore, many passages in the New Testament were derogatory to the character of God.[21] The treatise was likewise characterized by its anti-clerical spirit. The priesthood " had universally found the secret of living in tranquility amidst the anarchy they occasioned; secure under the despotism they sanctioned; in indolence amidst the industry they recommended; and in abundance in the very bosom of scarcity; and all this, by . . . selling words and gestures to the credulous. . . ." [22]

In his *Observations on the Increase of Infidelity* (1797), the English chemist, Priestley, then residing in America, upbraided Volney for his " inaccuracy " in dealing with the ancient Hebrew religion and with Jesus.[23] Charging that the Frenchman was either ignorant of the truth or misrepresenting it, the English Unitarian demanded an answer to

Campbell, *Evidence of Christianity; A Debate* (Cincinnati, 1852), p. viii (Introduction). *The New Harmony Gazette* printed the significant deistic passages of Volney's work (December 26, 1827, January 9, 16, 23 and 30, 1828 and February 6, 1828 [nos. 12-17 inclusive]).

[20] Volney attributed the ruin of these great states to the desire for gain which led to tyranny and slavery. As a result of these two abuses, the natural rights of man were infringed upon and the ancient empires disappeared.

[21] Volney, *Ruins, etc.* (New York, 1796), pp. 152-6, 163-6, 288-9.

[22] *Ibid.*, pp. 295-6. See also pp. 81, 293-4.

[23] Priestley, *Observations, etc.*, pp. 111-4, 118-20.

his accusations. Upon his arrival in Philadelphia (1797), Volney refused to enter into any serious discussion with Priestley because he felt that the Englishman had not assailed the *Ruins* but had merely attacked him. Persuaded that a controversy would be futile, the deist asked only to be left alone.[24]

In the meantime, another deist attempted to destroy traditional Christianity. Elihu Palmer was one of the most important deists produced in America. Forced to resign from a Baptist Church in Philadelphia because of his heterodox views and prevented from holding meetings because of the hostility of the clergy, the blind preacher was ready to accept the challenge of the French Revolution. He proposed to save liberalism from despotism by destroying that powerful ally of the throne—the clergy. Like Paine, he set out to accomplish this purpose by doing away with revealed religion. In 1793, Palmer, announcing the dawn of "the age of reason and philosophy", thought that the time had arrived for the advent of a "pure and unadulterated morality" stripped of all "mysteries and external trappings. . . ."[25] Some years later, in his *Principles of Nature,* he endeavored to offer such a system of ethics. While his friends enthusiastically acclaimed this pamphlet as a certain guide to "the path of Truth and Virtue", his enemies bitterly condemned it as an excellent example of how wretched and comfortless a thing deism was.[26]

In his *Principles of Nature,* Palmer sought to divorce

[24] Volney, *Answer to Dr. Priestley* (Philadelphia, 1797), pp. 4-9, 12-3.

[25] *Political Miscellany, etc.* (New York, 1793), pp. 22, 26. For Palmer's life see *Posthumous Pieces . . . To which are Prefixed a Memoir . . . by his friend John Fellows, etc.* (London, 1824).

[26] Contrast *The Temple of Reason,* February 19, 1803, vol. ii, p. 407 with the *American Review and Literary Journal,* October, November and December, 1801 (no. 4), vol. i, pp. 448-59.

morality from theology and consequently was led to assail the dogmas and divine revelation of Christianity. The doctrines of the Trinity, the immaculate conception, and original sin were discarded as absurd and immoral. Christian miracles were also rejected because many of them were not accepted by those living at the time of Jesus. Since some of the prophecies of Christianity had not been fulfilled, they likewise were repudiated. Naturally Palmer denied the divine authority of the Bible and therefore looked to " the nature of man " for the basis of his ethical system. Although such a system could not be categorically set forth, it was best exemplified in the " pure and holy religion " of " Theism " or deism. This " faith " declared " the existence of one perfect God . . . [and] the practice of a pure, natural, uncorrupted virtue. . . ." Built upon this creed, deism would flourish long after " Christian superstition and fanaticism " were forgotten.[27]

The deism of Paine, Volney and Palmer, presented in a popular form, was designed to reach the masses in order to destroy their faith in traditional Christianity with its priesthood, dogmas and supernatural revelation. Its ultimate end was to replace the Christian religion by the religion of nature with its three-fold creed—God, virtue and immortality, a creed believed in even by devout Christians. To popularize the teachings of " the new faith ", societies, lectureships and newspapers were established to supplement the writings of

[27] Palmer, *Principles of Nature* (London, 1823), pp. 8, 10-16, 30-3, 35-7, 42, 67-8, 85. Although Palmer looked upon theism and deism as synonymous terms, they are not necessarily so regarded to-day. After showing how theism is different from atheism, polytheism, pantheism and how it is similar to deism, *The Shorter Oxford English Dictionary* (Oxford, 1933) states, " Belief in one God as creator and supreme ruler of the universe, without denial of revelation; in this use distinct from *deism*." (See also Funk and Wagnalls, *New Standard Dictionary of the English Language* [New York, 1933], p. 2497).

Paine, Palmer and Volney. The first of these agencies was the most important cog in the deistic missionary machine because it was used to distribute skeptical treatises, to initiate discussions and to raise funds. The collection of money was, however, a difficult matter because these organizations were largely supported by the poorer classes—artisans, booksellers and printers—whose financial resources were limited. Of the learned professions, physicians alone were represented.[28]

In 1790, a deistic club, the Universal Society, was founded in Philadelphia under the guidance of John Fitch, one of the early inventors of a steamboat. Feeling that Christians were not adhering to their professed beliefs, Fitch drifted into the deistic current. He was especially disgusted with the Methodist denomination of which he was a member. During the Revolutionary War, his Trenton brethren censured him because he worked on Sundays to supply the American forces with arms. His repugnance reached a climax when leading Methodists refused to see him upon his arrival at New York in 1782. Fitch became an avowed disbeliever and, under his guidance, the Universal Society adopted a series of skeptical questions for its weekly discussions. Was there any religion which could be framed useful to society? If so, what were its principles? Was there a Providence? Did a future state exist? A strict moral code was instituted to guide the lives of the organization's thirty members. In 1791, the Universal Society joined Elihu Palmer who was then holding his religious services in the Church Alley meeting-house. In his sermons, the minister denied the divinity of Christ with such force that the Episcopal Bishop of Philadelphia, White, used his influence to prevent the owner of the building from allowing Palmer and his congregation to continue their assemblies. In view

---

[28] Koch, *Republican Religion*, pp. 290-1.

of this situation, the society came to an end after a year's activity.[29]

Philadelphia soon had another deistic organization in the form of a Theophilanthropic Society. The militant skepticism of this club was reflected in a discourse delivered before it and reprinted in *The Temple of Reason* for May 27 and June 3, 1801. In this speech, the lecturer urged the formation of more deistic societies where skeptical Christians might rally in order to save their neighbors from the chains of superstition. He encouraged his hearers to promote deism and at the same time launch a movement to revise the system of property holdings. Property was to be acquired on the basis of natural justice which left no room for greed. Without realizing it, the speaker was a prophet of the future because succeeding deists formed freethinking organizations and associated themselves with Owenite socialism.

Meanwhile, Palmer, with the aid of some members of a local democratic club established a deistic society in New York. In 1794, a group of New Yorkers founded an organization devoted to the spread of French revolutionary principles. This body was soon joined by the members of an older democratic order, Tammany. In the same year (1794), the newly organized radical society asked Palmer, who was then visiting the city, to deliver a speech before its members. Some of the latter were deeply impressed and proposed to aid the blind clergyman. For this purpose, a Deistical Society was founded during the winter of 1796-7. The name was suggested by the militant Palmer who desired to advocate frankly deistic principles and consequently refused to hide behind the harmless appellation of theophilanthropy. Moreover, Palmer himself drew up its consti-

---

[29] T. Westcott, *Life of John Fitch* (Philadelphia, 1878), pp. 302, 308-9; and Scharf and Westcott, *History of Philadelphia* (Philadelphia, 1884), vol. ii, pp. 1404-5 (note).

tution which consisted of a number of principles proclaiming the existence of God, the moral and intellectual sufficiency of man, the necessity of political and religious liberty and the universality of natural religion. Since the association sought to promote " moral science " and the religion of nature, its members were urged to oppose " all schemes of superstition and fanaticism, claiming divine origin." [30] The organization was divided into a number of grades and since secrecy was prescribed, the members of one grade did not know those of another. The meetings were closed; at these gatherings Christianity was ridiculed and Palmer's *Principles of Nature* read. On the whole, the society was far from being successful; it was unable to attract the " sober and substantial " elements of the community. From a financial viewpoint, it was forever in difficulties; one of its chief sources of revenue was the payment of membership dues. In 1802, these amounted to six cents payable at each meeting, a rather modest contribution which was probably fitted to the financial status of these " ' scattered dregs of . . . Jacobin Infidels.' " Yet, in spite of its monetary embarrassments, the association was for a time able to support the publication of *The Temple of Reason* under the editorship of Dennis Driscol, a recent Irish immigrant and ex-priest. Besides financial difficulties, there were political ones; at the turn of the century, the society became involved in New York politics on the ground that members of the Clintonian faction were at the same time members of the association. The exact connection of De Witt Clinton, later vice-president of the American Bible Society, with Palmer's deistical organization is not clear but it has been established that David Denniston, his cousin, was one of its members. [31] With the

---

[30] E. Palmer, *Posthumous Pieces . . . To which are prefixed . . . Mr. Palmer's Principles of the Deistical Society of New York*, pp. 8-9, 12.

[31] Koch, *Republican Religion*, pp. 76-7, 80, 84-5, 98, 100, 103.

death of Palmer in 1805, the deistic club languished; a few years later the remnants of the Old Guard formed a Society of Theophilanthropy in whose official organ, *The Theophilanthropist,* the posthumous works of Paine appeared.

Unlike the New York deistic society, the Newburgh organization drew its membership from the more " respectable " elements of the community; for example, doctors of medicine, like Dr. Hedges, were connected with it. The Druidical Society of Newburgh was an offshoot of an earlier and more conservative organization. In 1788, a Masonic lodge was founded which developed along radical lines during the course of the French Revolution. From its membership the Druidical Society was formed. The new body continued to use not only the ceremonies of the Masonic order but its former meeting place. In adopting the name Druid, these apostate Masons believed that they were returning to the pure worship of the sun from which both Christianity and Freemasonry were derived. At their weekly meetings, the Bible was openly ridiculed. Like the New York deists, the Druids fell under the influence of Palmer who lectured before them and was offered a salary by them. The society reprinted Paine's *Age of Reason* and Tindal's *Christianity as Old as the Creation* both of which it diligently circulated. After 1800, it declined in importance; the last notice of its activities appeared in the Newburgh *Rights of Man* for September 17, 1804.[32] Like Newburgh, Baltimore possessed a deistic club in the form of a Theophilanthropic Society, while the newly settled region west of the Genesee River in New York State also boasted of a freethinking association with a circulating library containing the writings of Voltaire, Volney, Hume and Paine.[33]

[32] *Ibid.,* pp. 118-9, 122-3, 129; Ruttenber, *History of the Town of Newburgh,* pp. 87-9.

[33] *The Temple of Reason,* October 2, 1802, vol. ii, p. 251; Gillett, *His-*

Just as Palmer was connected with the activities of deistic societies, so was he associated with deistic lectures. From Newburgh to Atlanta, this apostle of missionary deism addressed enthusiastic audiences, the size of which varied in direct ratio to the sympathies of the reporter. Colonel John Fellows, editor of the New York *Beacon* and a friend of Palmer, Jefferson and Paine, stated that the former minister's addresses were well attended, while an unfavorable newspaper critic asserted that upon one occasion only fifty-four were to be found at a well-advertised lecture in New York.[34] Palmer was so superb a speaker that, according to a New York historian of the period, " none could be weary within the sound of his voice. . . ." Even an unfriendly contemporary, Hargrove, conceded the oratorical brilliance of the former clergyman.

His lectures were characterized by their poignant hostility toward traditional Christianity. On December 25, 1796, in a New York speech, Palmer rejected the divinity of Jesus as an event which was "very singular and unnatural. . . ." He also discarded the doctrines of original sin, atonement, faith and regeneration as immoral and incomprehensible. In subsequent addresses, Palmer showed New Yorkers that a miracle-working Providence was inconsistent with the nature of God and that " Christian superstition " was one of the worst banes in the history of mankind. He even had the audacity to censure Jesus for having cried on the cross that God had deserted him. The speaker claimed that this action showed a lack of philosophical firmness in the hour of death and an inability to work miracles when needed. Having

tory of the Presbyterian Church (Philadelphia, 1864), vol. ii, p. 109 and J. H. Hotchkin, *A History of the Purchase and Settlement of Western New York* (New York, 1848), p. 26.

[34] Palmer, *Posthumous Pieces*, etc., p. 8 and the *Balance and Columbian Repository*, November 22, 1803 (no. 47), vol. ii, p. 372.

been invited by the deists of Baltimore to address them, Palmer continued to hurl his shafts of criticism at revealed religion in general and Christianity in particular.[35] So distinctly anti-Christian were his speeches that upon one occasion he was temporarily prevented from delivering one of them. In July 1801, he was asked to address the Universalist Church in Philadelphia on the subject of morality. A large audience gathered at the meeting-house but Palmer was not allowed to speak. A month later, however, he addressed a large and attentive assembly in the same city upon the same subject.[36] Another deistic orator aided Palmer in an endeavor to spread the gospel of natural religion. The speeches of John Foster were even more daring than those of his blind co-worker whom he addressed as brother. Foster, who probably taught Palmer theology at Pittsfield in 1787, was hailed in New York during the years 1803-06 as a brilliant orator and keen thinker. His speeches were especially well received by the skeptically inclined.

An attempt was made to propagate deism not only by lectures designed to reach the masses but also by newspapers aimed to popularize freethinking arguments. On November 8, 1800, *The Temple of Reason* appeared with the announcement that it proposed to show the purity and soundness of deistic doctrines by " exposing . . . the corruption of those of our adversaries. . . ." For more than two years, it sought to fulfill its aim by vigorously assailing Christian dogmas and evidences.[37] Adopting such a position, the

---

[35] These speeches were reported and refuted by Hargrove, editor of *The Temple of Truth*, an orthodox Baltimore periodical. See *ibid.*, September 5 and 12, 1801 (nos. 5 and 6), pp. 65-8, 81-91. Consult also *Temple of Reason*, August 26 and September 9, 1801, vol. i, pp. 263, 278-9.

[36] *Temple of Reason*, July 18, August 12 and 26, 1801, vol. i, pp. 207, 247, 262-3.

[37] *Temple of Reason*, December 3, 1800, vol. i, pp. 45-6, January 7, 1802,

newspaper urged all deists to cast prudence aside and boldly proclaim their support of deism. It also advised them to join theophilanthropic societies in order to revive " true morality ". In view of the fact that the appearance of *The Temple of Reason* coincided with the election of Jefferson to the presidency, religious and political conservatives had the opportunity of circulating the rumor of a carefully arranged plot to stamp out religion. Making as much of the opportunity as possible, they spread the report that *The Temple of Reason* was seeking the patronage and protection of the " atheistic President." In its issue of May 3, 1801, the accused newspaper felt called upon to deny the rumor by asserting that deism differed from " a religion of dreams and fables, of whales and asses, [and] of pigeons and strumpets " in that it was not dependent on state aid for success.

In the meantime, a Baltimore clergyman, John Hargrove, published *The Temple of Truth* to serve as an antidote to the influence of the deistic newspaper. Since *The Temple of Reason* refused to print some of his articles, Hargrove established a journal which would circulate his views and those of other orthodox believers.[38] The new periodical appeared in August 1801 and naturally defended the cause of Christianity. Its articles pointed out the advantages of the Christian religion in contrast to the disadvantages of deism. Besides, they sought to uphold the divine origin of the Old Testament and the utility of the Christian doctrine of patience.[39] The latter was defended because the more patient the man the better the reasoner; the better the reasoner the

vol. i, p. 409 and July 24, 1802, vol. ii, pp. 201-3. For the newspaper's deistic profession of faith see *ibid.*, November 8, 1800, vol. i, pp. 1-2 and July 31, 1802, vol. ii, pp. 213-4.

[38] See *The Temple of Truth*, August 1 and 15, 1801 (nos. 1 and 2) and *The Temple of Reason*, July 1 and 15, 1801, vol. i, pp. 199, 214-5.

[39] *The Temple of Truth*, August 15 and 29, October 31, 1801 (nos. 2, 4, 13), pp. 25-6, 58-60, 205-6.

more virtuous the man. Popular support of the newspaper, however, waned to such an extent that it ceased publication after October 31, 1801. To console himself, its editor assigned its failure to the fact that its truths were too rational for the fanatic and too spiritual for the deist. Its rival, *The Temple of Reason,* commenting upon the fate of the orthodox newspaper, remarked jubilantly, " We fear that faith has fled the land, and that infidelity is going to take her place! "

Less than two years later, *The Temple of Reason* discontinued its activities because subscriptions were not paid promptly enough. In its last number, it informed its readers that Elihu Palmer intended to revive the newspaper and, on December 10, 1803, the first issue of the *Prospect, or View of the Moral World* appeared with the expressed purpose of investigating fully the divine nature of Christianity. Consequently, its editor, Palmer, wrote a series of articles which commented upon every chapter in the Old and New Testaments. Beginning with the first section of Genesis, he continued his work with such extreme minuteness that some forty-four subsequent editions of the *Prospect* were issued before he completed the thirty-fifth chapter of Exodus.[40] Palmer announced a plan to erect a Temple of Nature where one God would be worshipped. In order to facilitate the matter, a meeting was held at 89 Broadway, in New York, where $600 was subscribed. To secure more money another meeting was proposed,[41] and soon with the help of Paine a " Theistic Church " was founded. The expectations of an

[40] *Prospect, or View of the Moral World,* January 14 to November 17, 1804 inclusive (nos. 6 to 50). It is interesting to note that after his publication of *The Principles of Nature,* Palmer desired to publish in pamphlet form his views on every chapter of the Bible (Palmer, *Posthumous Pieces, etc.,* p. 9).

[41] *Ibid.,* August 18 and 25, 1804 (nos. 37 and 38), pp. 296, 304.

organized deistic movement were given a temporary setback when the *Prospect* was discontinued on March 30, 1805 because of financial difficulties.   The extent of its circulation is somewhat revealed by the fact that its subscribers were requested to pay their money to Dr. Hedges in Newburgh, to Mr. Spalding in Rhinebeck, to Mr. Miles in Philadelphia and to Mr. Palmer in New York.

While this organized deistic movement was being launched, a deistic liberal, Jefferson, was elected to the presidency. Throughout the campaign of 1800, the Republican candidate was vilified by political and religious conservatives who charged him and his party with the desire to overthrow Christianity.   That this accusation was groundless is seen in the fact that the leadership of the Republican group represented all shades of religious opinion.   On the left, were Jefferson, Willie Jones and Freneau whose approach to the question of the Christian revelation was most prudent.   For instance, Philip Freneau, editor of *The National Gazette,* felt called upon as a good republican to defend the principles of the French Revolution from clerical destruction.   Although bitterly condemning the clergy, especially the Congregational order of New England, he nevertheless did not, like Palmer, reject explicitly the Biblical basis of ecclesiastical pretensions to authority.   In his *Letters on Various Interesting and Important Subjects* (1799), Jefferson's friend assailed religious dogmas on the ground that they promoted discord.   Moreover, he argued that the practice of orthodoxy was impossible because ministers were constantly changing their positions.   To illustrate his contention, he pointed out that for two hundred years the American ministry had been praying for the downfall of the Pope but now seemed anxious to see his power restored in France.   Cynically he advised Calvinistic clergymen to sail to that " unfortunate country " and there preach gospel sermons to unhappy Frenchmen.   In the same sarcastic vein, Freneau told how a school boy once misread the New Testament text to the effect that there would be "whipping and slashing to death" instead of the original "weeping and gnashing of teeth". Commenting upon this, he asserted that the boy had nearly preserved the sense of the passage and even if he had not, it did not matter.[42]

More to the right, were Sullivan and Barlow whose position was that of religious liberals. James Sullivan, a member of Brattle Street Church, Boston, used his influence in 1802 to secure the appointment of a Unitarian clergyman, Joseph Buckminister, whose religious opinions coincided with his own. Sullivan believed in the divine authenticity of the Bible but repudiated the Trinitarian doctrine. Moreover, he was persuaded that what the various churches held in common was more important than their disagreements. Although charged with being a deist and atheist, Joel Barlow, according to his own testimony, was neither. The famous American poet was made a citizen of France because of the active part which he played in the French Revolution. While in Europe, he was on intimate terms with Paine whose *Age of Reason* he helped to publish and with Volney whose *Ruins* he translated. His epic poem, *The Columbiad,* appeared in 1807, two years after his return to America. Two of his friends, Noah Webster and the Abbé Gregoire immediately assailed him as an atheist. When the orthodox joined in the attack, Barlow was forced to state explicitly his religious views. In a letter, written in 1809, he emphasized the point that at no time during the Revolution had he embraced either deism or atheism. He denied that his *Columbiad* was designed to ridicule or insult "the Christian system, as inculcated in the Gospels and explained by the Apostles. . . ." Furthermore, since the religious views of men depended upon the place of their birth, he, being born and educated among

[42] Freneau, *Letters, etc.* (Philadelphia, 1799), pp. 35-6, 72-5, 79.

Puritans, was still a Presbyterian.   Had he been reared in
Constantinople, the probability would be that he would adhere
to the Moslem faith.[48]   To the right of Barlow and Sullivan,
were such religious conservatives as Samuel Adams of
Massachusetts and William Findley of Pennsylvania whose
orthodoxy and political liberalism were beyond question.

In a similar fashion, the Federalist leadership represented
diverse religious views.   John Jay, Fisher Ames and Alexander Hamilton were all sincerely attached to the Christian
religion and vigorously opposed to deistic innovations.   Jay
scrupulously observed the customs of the Episcopalian
church.   The New York governor attended services regularly, was responsible for the erection of a house of worship,
and felt that the support of the clergy was a duty obligatory
upon all Christians.   When the American Bible Society was
formed, he became its president.   This organization was
responsible in no small measure for the decline of deism.
To Jay, "mere human reason" was incapable of acquiring
sufficient knowledge to inform men either of their actual or
future state.   Again, Biblical mysteries were to be accepted,
since they could never be understood by the "light of
reason".   That the Hebraic revelations were carefully preserved, that Jesus fulfilled the prophecies of the Old Testament and that he performed miracles which were faithfully
recorded—these tenets were accepted by Jay without question.
According to him, deism failed to accomplish its sinister
designs because the people were shocked by the tactics of its
disciples.   Like Jay, Ames was a firm believer in the divine
origin of the Christian religion and upon one occasion made
a public profession of faith.   The Christian system being
"excellent and benign . . .", the Massachusetts Federalist

[48] Todd, *Life and Letters of Joel Barlow* (New York, 1886), pp. 222-
232; Hazen, *Contemporary American Opinion of the French Revolution*
(Baltimore, 1897), p. 224 and the *Dictionary of American Biography*, vol.
i, pp. 611-2 (Article on Joel Barlow).

never troubled himself with subtle theological difficulties. Moreover, he was persuaded that these related to insignificant and uncertain points. Similarly, Alexander Hamilton strongly supported the cause of religion which appeared to him to be essential to stability in government. Deism was an " hideous " monster which had to be crushed.[44]

Yet, among the leaders of Federalism there were at least three distinguished religious liberals, Timothy Pickering, John Adams and Josiah Quincy. At Harvard, Pickering came in contact with the latitudinarian views of Tillotson whose works he was urged to read but was cautioned against their "heresies". He soon began to doubt his Puritan theology going even so far as to question the Trinitarian doctrine. This he did during the Revolutionary War when he heard von Steuben say that he would sooner believe in an absurdity than in the Trinity. In time, Pickering became a Unitarian who accepted the existence of one God, Governor of the World, and of one Mediator, Jesus, who " ' gave himself as a ransom for all ' ". Every Christian was to do those things which he believed the Deity enjoined. Persons who espoused the Christian religion could not be said to be credulous, since Boyle, Locke and Newton were among its sincere believers. Furthermore, the Old and New Testaments were divinely inspired.[45]

On the question of the validity of the Christian revelation, John Adams was a trifle more skeptical than Timothy Pickering. To the second President of the United States, the disclosures of nature were to be trusted to a greater degree

[44] Hazen, *Contemporary American Opinion of the French Revolution,* p. 266; F. Ames, *Works,* ed. S. Ames (Boston, 1854), vol. i, pp. 25-6; and W. Jay, *Life of John Jay* (New York, 1833), vol. i, pp. 13, 253, 434, 461, 463, 495-505 (Appendix, no. iv).

[45] Pickering and Upham, *Life of Timothy Pickering* (Boston, 1867), vol. i, pp. 11 (note), 35-6, vol. ii, p. 283, vol. iv, pp. 325-6 and Schneider, *Puritan Mind,* pp. 203-4.

than the Biblical testimony of miracles and prophecies. Although accounts of supernatural predictions and events could be used to frighten men, they could never make them believe that "two and two [are] five. . . ." Yet, in spite of his skeptical tendencies, Adams did not reject Christianity but actually supported it as an indispensable aid to stability in government. Therefore, as far as he was concerned, the deism of Paine was to be fought, since it promoted " the cause of revolution. . . ." [46] In short, the conservatism of Adams overcame his intellectual radicalism and forced him to remain within the limits of religious propriety.

Like Adams and Pickering, Josiah Quincy was a native of Massachusetts, a prominent Federalist leader and a religious liberal with distinct Unitarian inclinations. The President of Harvard opposed all theological controversies because they tended to divide rather than unite Christians. To him, it was of little consequence what a man thought so long as he acted according to the principles and sanctions of Christianity. These were essential to knowledge which in turn was basic to virtue. Virtue led to freedom; freedom to happiness. Moreover, Quincy held that religion had no reference to place and that true goodness would always conform to nature.[47]

Probably more of a freethinker than any of these three New Englanders was Charles Cotesworth Pinckney who was charged with being a deist during the campaign of 1800.

[46] Although these observations of Adams were taken from letters written after 1805, they represent to all intents and purposes his position on religion during the last decade of the eighteenth century. J. Adams, *Works*, ed. C. F. Adams, vol. ix, p. 627 (Letter to Benjamin Rush, January 21, 1810) and P. Wilstach, *Correspondence of John Adams and Thomas Jefferson* (New York, 1925), pp. 80-5 (Letter of September 14, 1813).

[47] J. Walker, *Memoir of Josiah Quincy* (Massachusetts Historical Society *Proceedings* [Boston, 1867], vol. ix, pp. 155-6).

This accusation was based upon a statement made by Dwight in his *Triumph of Infidelity*. Besides this " proof ", another one was presented by the anonymous author of *Serious Facts, Opposed to ' Serious Considerations '*, etc. This proof consisted of the testimony of Dr. William Linn to the effect that Pinckney was a deist. It is interesting to note that Linn was the author of *Serious Considerations,* a pamphlet directed against Jefferson's " open profession of Deism ".[48] Like Pinckney, William Davie was a southerner and a prominent Federalist. Born in England, he was taken to America in 1763 where he was adopted by a Presbyterian clergyman who saw to it that he received a collegiate education. During the Revolution, he rendered distinguished military services and after the struggle, settled in the borough of Halifax which he represented in the North Carolina legislature almost continuously from 1786 to 1798. As a recognized leader of the state's Federalist forces, Davie bitterly fought " that man " Jefferson as well as all Republican principles. In spite of his conservative politics, he was, as one of his biographers puts it, " infected with the infidelity of his times, [and] was never in any sense a religious man ",[49] although his actions were highly moral and his character unassailable. Thoroughly distrusting clergymen, he opposed the selection of a Scotch-Irish Presbyterian McCorkle as President of the University of North Carolina because nothing went well so long as " these men of God " had a " hand in it ". In place of McCorkle, David Ker, who later became an avowed skeptic, was chosen. Moreover, Davie did not hold the Bible in

---

[48] Marcus Brutus, *Serious Facts, Opposed to ' Serious Considerations':* *Or the Voice of Warning to Religious Republicans* (New York [?], 1800), pp. 10-11, 14; Linn, *Serious Considerations on the Election of a President* (New York, 1800), p. 4.

[49] J. G. de R. Hamilton, *William Richardson Davie, A Memoir, etc.* (in U. of N. C. James Sprunt Historical Monograph, No. 7, p. 22).

high esteem. When the wife of one of his friends died, he did not try to console the bereft husband with texts taken from Christian origins but, in characteristic deistic fashion, quoted Mohammedan sources.

The leaders of Republicanism and Federalism represented all shades of religious thought but the contemporary belief, especially of New England, was that all Jeffersonians were champions of deism and all Federalists defenders of orthodoxy. In the words of one New England newspaper, Jefferson and his associates were " philosophical infidels " who were plotting to usher in "the heretic ' Age of Reason '. . . ." Yet, these sinister men were being supported by stern Presbyterians, Baptists and Methodists! In Connecticut and Massachusetts, the Republican Party drew its main support from members of these last two denominations who assailed the Federalist Congregational order on the ground that a state church maintained by forced contributions led to the rise of freethinking. Elder John Leland, a Baptist clergyman who played an important role in the evangelical movement, made this quite clear in a sermon delivered in 1801. This ardent adherent of Jeffersonianism held that the only way to prevent the spread of deism was for religion to renounce state aid and convince the world it could stand alone. In a like fashion, the Scotch-Irish of western Pennsylvania, though radical in politics, were conservatives in religion. Representing their position were such popular Republican leaders as William Findley and John Smilie. Findley was distinctly orthodox in his views; he was brought up with the Bible as his companion, was for many years an elder of the Presbyterian Church and, at the turn of the century, was willing to bolt the Jeffersonian Party rather than accept a gubernatorial candidate, Ross, reputed to be a deist. Likewise, his friend, Smilie supported the Presbyterian Church and, according to his biographers, was in the " truest sense a Christian." [50] In view of the religious conservatism of these supporters of the Republican Party, it is not surprising to note that after 1800 good Jeffersonians pointed with pride to the spread of revivalism as an ample refutation of the Federalist charge that a Republican victory would mean the advent of deism. In spite of contemporary accounts, Liberalism, not Religion, was at stake in 1800. Abraham Bishop, a New England leader of Jeffersonian democracy, was quite right in stating that at the turn of the century deists were to be found in both the Republican and Federalist parties.[51]

Contemporary public opinion in New England associated deism not only with the Republican movement but also with French influence. In his *Discourse on Some Events of the Last Century* (1801), Dwight pointed out that " infidelity " was accorded "an extensive reception" in America due chiefly to enthusiasm for the leaders of the French Revolution. Another New Englander, Seth Payson, wrote in 1802 that the " principles of infidelity have attended the progress of French influence. . . ." [52] Yet, in spite of these observations, the deistic movement in America was scarcely influenced by that of France. An interest in things French was greatly stimulated by the French Revolution and a Francophile spirit characterized the followers of Jefferson. A

[50] McMaster and Stone, *Pennsylvania and the Federal Constitution* (Lancaster, 1888), pp. 727-9, 753; Albert, *History of the County of Westmoreland, Pa.* (Philadelphia, 1882), pp. 208-11; *Dictionary of American Biography*, vol. vi, pp. 385-6; Lewis and Veech, *The Monongahela of Old* (Pittsburgh, 1892), p. 148; Robinson, *Jeffersonian Democracy in New England* (New Haven, 1916), pp. 41, 129-34, 136; Purcell, *Connecticut in Transition* (Washington, 1918), p. 31 and J. Leland, *Blow at the Roots* (New London, 1801), p. 29.

[51] Koch, *Republican Religion*, pp. 127-8, 262, 275.

[52] Dwight, *Discourse on Some Events of the Last Century* (New Haven, 1801), pp. 19, 32; Payson, *Proofs of the Real Existence, etc.*, p. 214.

majority of Republicans, however, were not pleased with the religious experiments of the Revolution and consequently apologized for or condemned them. Some sympathizers with France attempted to explain away the irreligious tendency of her leaders. The *National Gazette* for March 27, 1793 held that aristocracy was more dangerous than deism or atheism because it oppressed the moral and physical faculties of men. Moreover, the article pointed out that deists or atheists did not request the aid of rich and cruel priests.

Other supporters of France, instead of approving the activities of the revolutionaries, endeavored to show that the charge of irreligion was unfounded because the French constitution allowed peaceful assemblies for religious worship. Hard-pressed, these sympathizers seized upon the speeches of Godineau and Robespierre as evidences of the religious spirit of the French leaders. On November 20, 1793, Godineau, a tribune of the National Club of Bordeaux, delivered an address on the subject of religious worship. Taking his cue from Rousseau, he asserted that although the simple teachings of Jesus surpassed all others, they were distorted by mysteries and miracles. He urged all Frenchmen to spread the true gospel of Christ which appeared to him to be the gospel of the " sans-culotte." [53] In the same vein, in April 1794, Robespierre addressed the National Convention on the necessity of instituting the Worship of the Supreme Being.[54] In order to save France from " stupid " and " perverse " atheists and money-mad priests, the Incorruptible advised the

[53] That the basis of this speech is to be found in the teachings of Rousseau may be seen if one compares the *Social Contract*, tr. Cole (London, 1913), book iv, chapter viii, pp. 113-22 with Godineau's address reprinted in *The Temple of Reason*, September 16 and 23, 1801, vol. i, pp. 286-9, 296.

[54] Mathiez in his *Fall of Roberspierre* shows that this speech was based on a report made by Mathieu, a deputy of Oise, who first proposed such a worship. Mathiez, pp. 93-5.

initiation of public festivals dedicated to the Deity. These celebrations were designed to inculcate respect for laws, enthusiasm for liberty and love for one's country. On June 8, 1794, Robespierre himself officiated at the Parisian festival and in a brilliant speech informed his audience that republicans were alone worthy of adoring " the Being of Beings, Author of Nature . . ." who created men to love one another and attain happiness. After bitterly denouncing fanaticism and atheism, he called upon the French sans-culottes to free the world from tyranny. These speeches were reported in American newspapers [55] and as far as the *Independent Chronicle* for July 24, 1794 was concerned, it was impossible to believe that after Robespierre's speech anyone could accuse France of being atheistic or irreligious. While some Republicans were defending the religious policy of the revolutionaries, others felt that France had gone astray in this particular. Most conspicuous among these was Governor Samuel Adams of Massachusetts who, in his Fast Day proclamation of 1794, implored God to inspire France with a spirit of wisdom and true religion.

Unlike Adams, a small group of Republicans, headed by Paine and Palmer, was pleased with the attacks of French leaders upon religion. Capitalizing the interest stimulated by the Revolution for things French, this faction sought to promote the cause of deism by using the writings of French freethinkers. Consequently, the works of Voltaire, Rousseau and Volney [56] were reprinted in deistic newspapers

[55] For Godineau's speech see *Salem Gazette*, June 22, 1794 (no. 406) and *Temple of Reason*, September 16 and 23, 1801. For those of Robespierre consult the *American Mercury*, August 4 and 11, 1794 (vol. xi, nos. 526-7) and *The Pennsylvania Gazette*, August 27, 1794 (no. 3345).

[56] For a reprint of Voltaire's writings see *Temple of Reason*, May 6 and June 24, 1801, vol. i, pp. 136, 189, May 1 and August 14, 1802, vol. ii, pp. 111, 227; for Rousseau's *Prospect, or View of the Moral World*, May 5 to November 17, 1804 (nos. 22-50); and for Volney *Temple of Reason*, January 31 to June 3, 1801.

and were distributed through deistic societies. To what extent these French authors, who were read in America, "caused" Americans to assume a more aggressive stand is problematic. Voltaire and Volney were undoubtedly sources of inspiration for exceedingly radical deists who felt called upon to discredit clerical pretensions to authority in order to preserve the principles of the French Revolution. They used an approach similar to that adopted by the Sage of Ferney, an approach whose explicit negations were not at all to the liking of most American deists, not to say of most Americans. In short, although French deists exerted some "influence" upon a relatively small section of the American public, their "influence" was greatly exaggerated by Dwight and Payson, who, because of their Federalist affiliations, viewed with alarm the rise of Jeffersonianism which they sought to check by using the French bugaboo.

Likewise, New Englanders saw in Freemasonry a powerful force stimulating the growth of a militant deistic movement and again their observations were far-fetched. Masonic lodges appeared in America during the early eighteenth century and gradually attracted quite a following. Their members greatly increased after the Revolution on account of the infiltration of many French societies and the enrollment of prominent war heroes. The names of Washington, Franklin, Warren, Madison and Lafayette unquestionably attracted members and with increased membership came increased influence.[57] The growing importance of Freemasonry was reflected in articles and poems appearing in the periodical press after 1783.[58] During

[57] Jones, *America and French Culture* (Durham, 1927), p. 398; Tatsch, *Freemasonry in the Thirteen Colonies* (New York, 1929), pp. 140-1; and Fosdick, *French Blood in America* (New York, 1906), pp. 386-7.

[58] Laudatory articles appeared in *The Gazette of the State of South Carolina*, May 27, 1784 (no. 2204); *Maryland Gazette or Baltimore*

the last quarter ot the eighteenth century, French lodges were also established in America. Among these were the Perfect Union Lodge, Boston (1781), Lodge Wisdom, Portsmouth, Virginia (1786), *L'Amenité,* Philadelphia (1797) and the Grand Orient and Union Lodges in New York. Likewise, the Harmonic and Friendship societies, founded in Boston in 1792 and 1793 respectively, were composed of a considerable French element.[59]

The formation of these French Masonic orders at first caused little alarm. At the turn of the century, however, the self-appointed guardians of American institutions sounded the tocsin and informed the people that Freemasonry in America was being corrupted by " illuminism " in the guise of French lodges. On August 25, 1798, a Connecticut periodical *The Religious Monitor, or Theological Scales* announced " a secret conspiracy of the Illuminati in league with corrupted Masons . . ." which proposed to root out religion in Europe and America. In the meantime, the Reverend Jedidiah Morse showed the German origin of Illuminism and spoke of its spread to the new Republic. Its rapid progress, he held, was due to the popularity of such " an unprincipled author " as Thomas Paine.[61] To the aid of

Advertiser, March 30, 1787 (no. 259) ; *American Museum or Repository,* June, 1787, vol. i, pp. 546-8; and *Providence Gazette, etc.,* February 21, 1795 (no. 1625). Extracts from Masonic books and addresses appeared in the *Christian's, Scholar's and Farmer's Magazine,* April and May, 1789, vol. i, pp. 84-5 and *American Museum or Repository,* June, 1789, vol. ii, 597-600; poems were published in *The American Universal Magazine,* January 9, 1797, vol. i, p. 65 and the *Literary Museum or Monthly Magazine,* March, 1797, p. 160.

[59] Fosdick, *French Blood in America,* pp. 389, 393, 395-6; Morse, *A Sermon, Exhibiting the Present Dangers, etc.* (Charlestown, 1799), pp. 34-7; S. Payson, *Proofs, etc.,* pp. 197-8; and V. Stauffer, *New England and the Bavarian Illuminati,* pp. 321-2.

[60] J. Morse, *ibid.,* pp. 12-3, 27, 34-7 and Stauffer, *ibid.,* pp. 229-239, 264-71, 288-303.

Morse came such redoubtable warriors as Dwight and Payson who assiduously damned Illuminism, Infidelity and political radicalism. In his *Proofs of the Real Existence and Dangerous Tendency of Illuminism* (1802), Payson asserted that Voltaire, D'Alembert, Frederick II and Diderot were the principal actors in a plot to overthrow " the adorable religion " of Christ. Especially did he warn the young against the dangers of Illuminism and he urged parents to teach their children " the fear of God . . . and the evidences of the Christian faith. . . ." Stating that there were 1700 agents of the Illuminati in America, he suggested the temporary suspension of Masonic lodges.[61]

Although American Freemasonry was not as anti-Christian as these statements would indicate, it nevertheless showed distinct deistic tendencies. By referring to God as " the Great Architect " and by alluding to natural religion, Masonic prayers and addresses familiarized Masons with deistic phraseology. Moreover, the Masonic charge that members were to comply with " the essentials of religion " rather than with Christian usages gave Masons an opportunity to embrace deism. Some of them, like those in Newburgh, went so far as to form deistic societies,[62] but these were the exceptions to the rule. On the whole, the American Masonic movement was far from being anti-Christian, in fact, Masons were requested to shun deism. *The Ahiman Rezon* of 1783, edited by William Smith upon the request of the Pennsylvania Grand Lodge, stated that good Masons could never " tread in the irreligious paths of the unhappy libertine, the deist or the stupid atheist." Although fifteen years later the Reverend Mr. Harris, chaplain of the Grand Lodge of Massachusetts, qualified the statement quoted by excluding

---

[61] Payson, *Proofs, etc.*, pp. 31-36, 55-6, 155-8, 198, 254, 275.
[62] See chapter v, p. 133.

the name deist,[63] he pointed out that both Christianity and Freemasonry desired the encouragement of charity and benevolence as well as of moral and social duties.   In order to protect themselves against the suspicion of being deistic, some grand lodges, like that of Maryland, went so far as to propose that no member be initiated within its jurisdiction who refused to believe that the Ten Commandments were divinely revealed.   This proposition was suggested in 1804. Some seven years before, the Reverend Mr. Harris challenged " the most severe critic, the most precise moralist, the most perfect christian to point out anything in [Masonic ideals] inconsistent with . . . pure religion. . . ." [64] Moreover, many respectable religious and political leaders were connected with the Masonic movement so that eventually the bubble of Illuminated Freemasonry burst.

Although these New Englanders were wrong in their belief that Masonry was scheming to overthrow Christianity, they were correct in their assumption that deism was spreading.   Doctors, teachers, artisans, farmers and social leaders were embracing the deistic philosophy of Paine and Palmer. According to one report, a young physician of Hadley, New York, " was personally acquainted with Thomas Paine [and] had embraced his infidel sentiments . . .", while another statement spoke of a teacher, described as D. R., who secured for himself the reputation of being " a zealous opposer of the gospel and a universal seducer of unwary " youth.   The clergyman Lyman Beecher, who as a young man dressed flax, told how boys around him read Paine and believed in him. In a similar manner, in the seats of the mighty, the leaders

[63] Compare the *Ahiman Rezon* (Philadelphia, 1783), p. 14 with T. M. Harris, ed., *Constitution of the Ancient and Honorable Fraternity of Free and Accepted Masons* (Worcester, 1798), p. 34.

[64] Harris, *Ignorance and Prejudice shewn to be the Only Enemies of Freemasonry* (Leominister, Massachusetts, 1797), p. 23.

of fashionable society openly ridiculed Christianity. In 1793, the artist Trumbull was asked to dine at Jefferson's home. Here he met a group of freethinkers who proceeded to poke fun at the doctrines and character of Jesus. Much to his exasperation and astonishment, the only one at the table besides himself who was willing to defend the Christian religion was a Jew named Franks.[65] At another party, held some four years later, James Kent, a Federalist in politics and future Chancellor of the State of New York, remarked that well-informed men were free from the " vulgar super- stitions " of the Christian religion. This information was apparently approved by those present among whom were William Dunlap, a playwright, William Johnson, a lawyer and Elihu Hubbard Smith, a physician. It is interesting to note that when Smith died one year later, his parents anxiously asked Dunlap and his friends whether their son had died a deist or not. Those to whom the question was put were happy to evade it by pointing out that Smith had passed away so suddenly that even had he desired to recant, he would have been physically unable to do so.[66] Besides the professional classes, army officers were stung by the deistic bumble-bee. In 1798, John Davis, a British traveler, met and spoke to Major Howe, a Revolutionary veteran and a member of the Order of Cincinnati. According to Davis, Howe, while a commanding officer at West Point, borrowed Gibbon's *Decline and Fall of the Roman Empire*. He read the work diligently and soon rejected the Christian revelation. So thorough was his repudiation of the Bible that Howe became a follower of Palmer.[67]

[65] Griswold, *The Republican Court* (New York, 1855), p. 312.

[66] Koch, *Republican Religion*, pp. 82-3.

[67] J. Davis, *Travels of Four Years and a Half in the United States of America during 1798, 1799, 1800, 1801 and 1802* (New York, 1909), pp. 22-3.

Yet, in spite of the alarmist accounts of the faithful and the exultant reports of the heterodox, the deism of the Paine school was far from being popular. That it did attract some attention was due to the noisy aggressiveness of a small band of militant deists and to the attention bestowed upon them by the clergy. The deistic Freneau hit the nail on the head when he remarked that *The Age of Reason* might not have achieved the popularity it did, had not the clergy written tracts answering it. These, he continued, were read by people, who, on turning to Paine, would realize how badly the Christian cause was handled by its " weak, yet conceited friends. . . ." [68] Like Communism in 1919, deism in late eighteenth-century America attracted an attention which was out of proportion to its actual influence. With this in mind, let us turn to our sources of information and use these as an index to, rather than an exact account of, the extent of skepticism.

From 1794, deism, aided by the popular pamphlets of Paine and Volney, made its way throughout the country. At Lebanon, New York, in 1795, few would profess Christianity; those who did believe in the divine origin of the Bible felt that the " fundamental doctrines of religion were disgustful." Again it was said that in Windham County, Connecticut, the majority of people were deists while no more than six individuals in Marlborough, Vermont, would make a public profession of faith; at one time, not a single person was even willing to declare himself a Christian.[69] Philadelphia was regarded as a center of " infidelity "; one traveler observed that the services of learned apologists were

[68] Freneau, *Letters on various Interesting and Important Subjects*, pp. 37-8.

[69] Larned, *History of Windham County, Connecticut* (Worcester, 1894), vol. ii, p. 221; *Connecticut Evangelical Magazine*, September and November, 1803, vol. iv, pp. 111, 179. See also Dwight, *Travels in New-England and New-York* (London, 1823), *passim*, for skepticism in Vermont.

needed there in order to check the progress of skepticism. In New York, the "astonishing growth of infidelity" was given as the cause of the death of several hundred people during the yellow fever epidemic. In 1796, the Methodist Episcopal Church recommended a day of fasting and prayer in order to turn back the swelling tide of deism.

From 1797 to 1800, according to contemporary opinion, the skeptical current swept forward so rapidly that Christianity itself seemed about to be engulfed in a sea of deistic oblivion. Although Dwight cheerfully estimated that "the friends of Revelation" outnumbered its enemies, Priestley felt called upon to publish a work designed to prevent the spread of freethinking. His *Observations on the Increase of Infidelity* (1797) assigned two penetrating reasons for the ultimate defeat of deism—the absence of an established church in America and the inertia of the masses. Yet the immediate danger of deistic success was apparently so great that the General Assembly of the Presbyterian Church issued a solemn warning to the American people. In its Philadelphia meeting of 1798, the assembly predicted that unless Americans turned away from deism, the wrath of God would be visited upon them. To avert the impending day of doom, it was suggested that a day of humiliation, prayer and fasting be set aside. In the same vein, a writer in an orthodox magazine warned the people against " infidelity " which was raising " her presumptuous voice among both sexes and [leveling] her artillery against divine revelation. . . ." [70] These dire admonitions evidently had little effect, for during the following year such diverse observers as Morse and

[70] T. Dwight, *Nature and Danger of Infidel Philosophy*, p. 64; Priestley, *Observations, etc.*, pp. xv (Preface), 143-4; *Religious Monitor or Theological Scales*, June 30 and August 25, 1798, pp. 50, 81-3; *The Theological Magazine*, March, April and May, 1798, vol. iii, pp. 186-90; and E. H. Gillett, *History of the Presbyterian Church* (Philadelphia, 1864), vol. i, pp. 296-8.

Freneau reported an increase in the number of freethinkers. To check "the awful prevalence of speculative and practical infidelity", the Congregational clergy of Massachusetts urged the initiation of positive and vigorous action.[71]

As in Massachusetts, so in North Carolina, freethinking was causing great anxiety among the faithful. Joseph Caldwell, President of the University of North Carolina, found religion "'little in vogue'" and noted that in the region east of Chapel Hill, politicians, in order to secure votes, had to disavow publicly the doctrines of the Bible. Surveying the scene with the same Federalist bias, Caldwell's predecessor, Harris, held that only around Salisbury could "true religion" be found (whatever the good Professor, who was a Unitarian, might mean by the phrase "true religion"). When the *Minerva*, in August 1800, described Jefferson as "a second-handed varnished Deist", the "Hermit of Wake" defended the deism of the Republican standard-bearer in the *Raleigh Register*. The deistic philosophy was adopted so extensively by the professional classes of the South that the General Assembly of the Presbyterian Church viewed with satisfaction the conversion of many of these people to the "doctrines of Christianity".[72]

While deism was spreading, the orthodox were setting in motion an evangelical movement. Their efforts in this direction were recorded in letters sent to magazines, communications which indicated the triumph of Christianity over deism. From Caldwell, New Jersey, came the consoling news that some "chiefs of the devil's kingdom" had em-

[71] *The Panoplist*, February, 1809, vol. i, pp. 402-5; Morse, *A Sermon, Exhibiting the Present Dangers, etc.*, p. 8 and Freneau, *Letters, etc.*, p. 36.

[72] *The Panoplist*, August, 1810, vol. iii, pp. 145-7; and Gilpatrick, *Jeffersonian Democracy in North Carolina* (New York, 1931), pp. 121-2. See also Williams, *Memoirs of the late Rev. Thomas Belsham* (London, 1833), p. 593.

braced the gospel, while Ontario County, New York, reported the conversion of a deist of long standing. "Infidelity" also stopped "its brayings" in Milton, New York, where "many of its hearers, (or rather its dupes) fell prostrate at the feet of the Redeemer whom they had impiously denied and blasphemed!" A similar, although decidedly less graphic, report arrived from Middletown, Vermont, where skeptics were said to be again embracing the doctrines of Jesus. In Providence, Rhode Island, the "Deist [was bowing] to our King, and [was hailing] Jesus as his rightful Lord, and divine lawgiver. . . ." While these "glad tidings" were circulating, Dwight announced that New England had escaped "the dreadful bondage of Infidelity, corruption and moral ruin . . ." thanks to the activities of her leaders and of her God.[73] In the face of these orthodox reports, the deistic *Temple of Reason* for October 16, 1802 asserted that there were more deists than Christians in America. Two years later, Palmer's *Prospect, or View of the Moral World* for June 16, 1804 declared more modestly, albeit more accurately, that there were "thousands and tens of thousands of deists in the United States and Europe. . . ."

Deism was prevalent not only along the Atlantic seaboard but also in the region west of the Alleghanies. Here, as in the case of most frontier settlements, a general indifference to religion flourished. In 1800, in the Ohio Valley country, one missionary observed that " only a small number of people openly professed an attachment to religion. . . ." Shellyville, Kentucky, was " destitute of the gospel . . .", while Blount County, Tennessee, was " cold and indifferent " to

---

[73] Dwight, *A Discourse on Some Events of the Last Century*, p. 34; *The Theological Magazine*, January, 1797, vol. ii, p. 233; *The New-York Missionary Magazine*, 1800, vol. i, p. 37; and *The Massachusetts Baptist Missionary Magazine*, September, 1803, May, 1804 and January, 1806, vol. i, pp. 17-8, 50-1, 180.

religion. People in the vicinity of Pittsburgh also showed little interest in " spiritual matters." [74]

This indifference to religion, however, did not necessarily mean that the people of the West were deists or skeptics. There were among them deeply religious men and women drawn from the ranks of God-fearing Presbyterians, Baptists and Methodists. Into the trans-Appalachian country they carried their Bibles and attempted to establish their own churches. In their log schoolhouses, their children used the Scriptures as a textbook and were taught to sing hymns and answer questions taken from religious catechisms. Moreover, sermons, church histories and Bibles were the books most commonly read in the new region.[75] Their apparent indifference toward religion often signified merely that they did not have the same opportunity of worshipping as did their eastern neighbors. Lacking a sufficient number of ministers and widely scattered throughout the countryside, they found it difficult to conduct religious exercises. That the majority did desire to do so was evidenced by the success of the evangelical movement in Kentucky, Tennessee and Ohio. Addressed as it was to their hearts, revivalism appealed more easily to the frontiersmen than did deism.

The capital of Kentucky, Lexington, was reputed to be a center of deistic speculation. Here John Bradford, publisher of the *Kentucky Gazette,* helped organize democratic clubs and Harry Toulmin, " a sycophantic satellite of Thomas Jefferson" and a member " of the Priestly [sic] lineage ", presided over Transylvania Seminary.[76] Founded

[74] *The New-York Missionary Magazine* for 1800, vol. i, pp. 120-2 and *ibid.,* for 1801, vol. ii, p. 238.

[75] C. Cleveland, *The Great Revival in the West, 1797-1805* (Chicago, 1916), pp. 10-1, 17, 28-9.

[76] D. C. Troxel, "French Deism in Kentucky, 1800" (see summary in American Society of Church History, *Bulletin 5,* July, 1929, pp. 4-5).

in 1783, this institution was at first dominated by Presbyterians. By 1794, their influence waned to such an extent that Toulmin, who was popular with the deistic element of Lexington, was appointed head of the seminary. In view of this situation, the Presbytery of Transylvania established the Kentucky Academy in 1797. The following year, the state legislature authorized the two rival institutions to unite under the name of the Transylvania University. The board of trustees, created by the Act of 1798, was soon divided into two groups, the Presbyterian faction favoring the practices of evangelicalism and the deistic supporting the cause of rationalism. As time passed, the number of Presbyterians serving on the board was so reduced that the freethinking groups secured control of the university's policies.[77]

As early as 1793, the Kentucky legislature dispensed with the services of a chaplain. Two years later, the Presbyterians set aside a day for fasting, prayer and humiliation in order to check the growth of freethinking. Yet, this remedy appeared to be of little avail since it was asserted that a majority of the people of Kentucky were " infidels " at the turn of the century.[78] Freethinking was likewise prevalent in western New York where the Bible was openly ridiculed and where deistic societies were established. In 1798, one traveler observed that this newly settled region was seriously infected with deism.

[77] The struggle between these two forces continued into the early nineteenth century and broke with full fury during the presidency of Horace Holley. Holley, a deist of the Jeffersonian type, was naturally assailed by the orthodox. Because of the agitation of the faithful he was forced to resign in 1827.

[78] Gillett, *History of the Presbyterian Church in the United States,* vol. i, p. 421.

CHAPTER VI

CHRISTIANITY DEFENDED: EARLY NATIONAL PERIOD
(1789-1805)

To one contemporary clergyman, it seemed that during the last decade of the eighteenth century " every appearance of religion [would] vanish, yea that our Zion must die without an helper and that infidels would laugh at her dying groans. . . ." To avert such a catastrophe, another advocate of religion urged " the real friends of Zion " to check " the spreading frenzy of [the] Infidel Philosophy. . . ." [1] Among those who sought to " save " Christianity none were more zealous than the college authorities whose tranquility was deeply disturbed by the skeptical drafts of the deistic whirlwind. At Rhode Island (Brown) College, Queen's (Rutgers) College and Union College, baccalaureate addresses were delivered to impress the graduating classes with the superiority of Christianity over " mere philosophy ". At the Rhode Island College commencement of 1795, the presidential discourse dealt exclusively with the necessity of the Biblical revelation as a guide to the good life, while the student oration of Amos Hopkins sought to minimize the importance of deism by indicating that it was merely a prelude to the universal establishment of Christianity. Eliphalet Nott of Union College delivered a graduation address in 1805 in which he endeavored to show most vividly the advantages of the Christian religion over deism.[2]

[1] *The Connecticut Evangelical Journal*, October, 1800, vol. i, p. 137 and *The Religious Monitor*, August 25, 1798, p. 25.

[2] *The Providence Gazette and Country Journal*, September 12, 1795 (no. 1654) ; *The Independent Chronicle and Universal Advertiser*, September 17, 1795 (xxvii, no. 1515) ; and Schmidt, *The Old Time College President* (New York, 1930), pp. 195, 202-3.

The authorities at Yale also attempted to save the souls of their students. During the years 1794-5, a young sophomore at the New Haven college, Lyman Beecher, declared that the majority of the members of the class entering before his were skeptics. These students addressed each other by the names of Voltaire, Rousseau and D'Alembert. The evidences of Christianity were debated not only outside of the institution but also within its walls, since the " Deistic controversy was an existing thing, and the battle was hot, the crisis exciting. . . ." In the Divinity class, conducted by the President of the College, the following questions were discussed: Was Revelation necessary? Was Moses the author of the Pentateuch?

Although Yale students doubted the courage of their faculty to assail deism openly, Timothy Dwight advanced to the attack in his baccalaureate address of 1797. Warning the undergraduate body to avoid the deistic philosophy, the President described it as vain, deceitful and contradictory; its doctrines " gross and monstrous "; its authors vicious and depraved. Voltaire was an atheist, Rousseau a thief, perjurer, fornicator and Tindal " infamous for vice in general, and the total want of principle. . . ." In a sudden burst of magnanimity, Dwight conceded that some deists were ingenious and learned fellows but could not be compared with such " sober " Christians as Bacon, Erasmus, Locke and Newton. Even though the contemporary world was favorably disposed towards freethinking, Christianity would triumph because the " weight of virtue has been wholly on [her] side. . . ." [3]

Although Dwight was extremely orthodox, the same could not be said for his faculty. Tutor Silliman, though not parading heterodox views, was regarded as a deist and did

[3] T. Dwight, *Nature and Danger, of the Infidel Philosophy* (New Haven, 1798), pp. 20-37, 39-42, 45-7, 58, 63, 82.

not profess himself to be a Christian until 1803 during which year a revival took place at Yale. Another member of the staff whose religious complacency had been broken by Hume was "converted" through the efforts of Dwight. The benign influence of the ubiquitous college President was further seen in the changing attitude of the student body. Students organized a Moral Society which sought to reclaim "lost souls" by debating such topics as the necessity of divine revelation and the truth of Biblical stories. The salutary effects of these discussions were probably responsible for a student poem delivered at the commencement exercises of 1797. The poem consisted of a rejection of Volney's contentions concerning the providence of God.

A deistic spirit prevailed in other colleges besides Yale. In 1794, William E. Channing, a student at Harvard, observed a decided tendency toward skepticism at the Cambridge seat of learning.[4] Here the deism of Paine was making such rapid progress that the authorities felt it necessary to present each student with a copy of Watson's *Apology for the Bible*.[5] At the same time, a Dudleian lecturer, Nathan Fiske, warned all undergraduates to avoid reading *The Age of Reason* because its author was a "daring insurgent" who was ever ready to disturb peace and order. Fairness of treatment and learned research were not to be expected of him. These were characteristic only of the work of Christian apologists. Deism was not only partisan and superficial but also foreign and futile. Its doctrines were imported into the United States and in spite of their apparent popularity they would not achieve their end since Christianity has "been, and ever will be, under the patronage

[4] W. H. Channing, *Life of William Ellery Channing* (Boston, 1880), p. 30.

[5] In 1791, the college authorities publicly banned Gibbon's *Decline and Fall of the Roman Empire*.

of the Almighty. . . ." [6]   It was said that at Dartmouth only one member of the class of 1799 was willing to admit publicly that he was a Christian.   It was not until 1801 that a permanent student's Religious Society was established at the college.   The same state of affairs existed at Bowdoin; here only one student was ready to state openly his belief in Christianity.   At Princeton, in 1799, there were, according to report, only three or four " pious " youths.[7]   Although these accounts were undoubtedly exaggerated, they nevertheless indicated the spread of deistic influence.   The authorities at Princeton attempted to fight the hydra of deism.   In 1802, its trustees, appealing for funds, informed all friends of religion that they intended to make the college "an asylum for pious youth, so that in this day of general and lamentable depravity, parents [might] send their children to it with every reasonable expectation of safety and advantage. . . ."   The trustees significantly added that this purpose would make the college many enemies.[8]   Provost John Mason of Columbia also endeavored to preserve his institution against the inroads of deistic attacks.   He had no patience with the sophistries of those rationalists who relied on " the light of nature."   A living faith in the merits of Christ was the only consolation of a troubled conscience.[9]

Down in the Southland, conditions at the University of North Carolina were such as to cause uneasiness among the faithful.   Opened in 1795, the college was presided over by

[6] Fiske, *A Sermon Preached, etc.*, September 7, 1796 (Boston, 1796), pp. 16-18.

[7] Koch, *Republican Religion*, pp. 243, 281; Dorchester, *The Problems of Religious Progress* (New York, 1881), p. 99.

[8] *Address of the Trustees of the College of New-Jersey, etc.* (Philadelphia, 1802), p. 4.

[9] Schmidt, *The Old Time College President* (New York, 1930), pp. 118, 189-90.

a well-read Presbyterian clergyman, David Ker, who proved himself to be such an " outspoken infidel " that he was forced to resign within a year. His wife, a steadfast Christian, burnt all his writings for fear that they would contaminate others. Ker was succeeded by Charles W. Harris, Tutor of Mathematics, who, though not a deist, was heterodox enough to reject the Trinitarian creed. In turn, he made way for another man—a young Princeton graduate, Joseph Caldwell. A firm believer in the evidences of Christianity, the new acting President found upon his arrival that his faculty included so many " infidels " that he was unable to converse with his own staff. He openly charged one of the instructors, Samuel A. Holmes, with believing in nothing and even questioning the existence of virtue. Holmes was originally a Baptist preacher who was probably at this time a Republican and who " indulged in the Voltairean, Tom Paine cant of the times . . ."; consequently he was assailed by the Federalist president of the college. Like the faculty, the student body was skeptical; one boy wrote home that the favorite book of his fellow students was Paine's *Age of Reason*. Student clubs purchased Locke's *Essay on Human Understanding,* Gibbon's *Decline and Fall of the Roman Empire,* and Helvetius' *On the Human Mind;* they also held debates on various religious subjects. Upon one occasion, a club voted that it was inconsistent with reason to love one's enemy as taught by Christianity.[10]

Deism was assailed not only in the colleges but also in the outside world where some of the faithful endeavored to show the irrationality of the deistic position. Among the first to feel the fury of the orthodox blast was Paine whose *Age of Reason* was inspired by a deep feeling of devotion for humanity. So profound was his love for mankind that his

[10] Battle, *History of the University of North Carolina* (Raleigh, 1907), vol. i, pp. 61, 66, 68-9, 80-1, 85, 91, 101, 105, 107, 114-5, 157.

work assumed a religious flavor and consequently it is not surprising to note that it was first published in America by a religious house as a religious book and was sold in Virginia along with the Bible by Parson Weems, Washington's old friend and biographer.[11]   Although time has reduced *The Age of Reason* to a comparatively moderate treatise, so far as its negations are concerned, in its own day it was the acme of radicalism.   Naturally the gauntlet which this deistic knight threw down was quickly taken up by an array of Christian pamphleteers who ran the gamut from the vituperative and bigoted Ogden to the moderate and scholarly Watson.   Most of the works written against *The Age of Reason,* though masquerading under the pretentious titles of Answers, were nothing but emotional diatribes directed against its author.   On the whole, Uzal Ogden and David Nelson added nothing new to the deistic controversy with the possible exception of a more extensive list of abusive terms which the orthodox could fling at Paine.   To Ogden, the deistic champion was a sot devoid of reason, " grossly ignorant " and totally unoriginal.   This last remark might well have been used against the good Ogden himself.   Believing in the depravity of man, he held that natural religion needed the aid of revelation.   Since many things existed which were beyond human comprehension, men were fortunate to have special messengers sent by the Supreme Being to disclose these " mysteries ".   Like Ogden, Nelson, who adopted the pseudonym of " A Delaware Waggoner ", vented his spleen upon Paine whom he pictured as deceitful, degenerate and wanting in knowledge.   Describing *The Age of Reason* as an impious and erroneous book, he was satisfied that his own work completely refuted all of its arguments.[12]

[11] Paine, *Works,* ed. Van der Weyde, *With a Life of Thomas Paine,* vol. i, pp. 401-2.

[12] U. Ogden, *Antidote to Deism,* vol. i, pp. 15, 18-9, 121-2, 124-6, 150-72,

The works of Thomas Williams and James Muir were in the same general category as those of Ogden and Nelson. In his *Age of Infidelity,* Williams defended the truth of Christian evidences on the ground that Jesus fulfilled in his life the prophecies of the Old Testament and confirmed his mission by miracles. After examining the specific objections of Paine, Williams was convinced that deistic principles would spread only among " the young, the gay and the voluptuous . . .", and that Christian truth would prevail. The Reverend Mr. Muir of Alexandria was likewise certain that Christianity would be victorious; but, in order to make its triumph surer, he wrote an *Examination of the Principles Contained in the Age of Reason.* Believing that Paine's work was a specimen of effrontery and ignorance, he gently admonished the deist to mend his ways. After defending vigorously revealed religion, the Presbyterian clergyman concluded that unbelief led inevitably to crime and pestilence.

On a higher rational and scholarly plane was Priestley's *Answer to Mr. Paine's Age of Reason.* To the English chemist, the deistic knight-errant seemed to know as little about " the writings of Voltaire and other better informed unbelievers . . ." as he did about the circumstances surrounding the resurrection of Christ and the influence of Christianity upon the Middle Ages. Moreover, the Englishman reminded Paine that " intelligent Christians " no longer believed such doctrines as the Trinity and that he was therefore unfair in loading Christianity with these " absurdities." [13] As indicated by this work, Priestley and other

184, 192-8, 201-5, 308-14, 319; vol. ii, pp. 112-3, 171, 259, 297; and D. Nelson, *Investigation of that False, and Fabuluous, and Blasphemous Misrepresentation of Truth, set forth by Thomas Paine,* pp. 10-1, 14, 17, 41, 45, 47.

[13] Priestley, *Answer to Mr. Paine's Age of Reason* (Northumberland, 1794), pp. v. (Preface), 59-61, 66, 69-70, 77-9; Muir, *Examination of*

eighteenth-century Unitarians agreed in many respects with the deists. Like the latter, they accepted the notion that religion must be rational, simple, tolerant and broad. Yet, the Unitarians differed from the deists on the two-fold question of revelation and Jesus. Whereas the champions of deism rejected implicity or explicitly the divine origin and truth of the Biblical accounts, the Unitarians of the eighteenth century accepted them. Hence Priestly, like Hazlitt before him,[14] was able to pity " unbelievers " and to deliver lectures on the evidences of revelation. Moreover, deists and Unitarians were unable to agree on the person of Jesus. Whereas the former looked upon Christ as a superb philosopher, the latter regarded him as more than a man, even though he was not a member of the Godhead. To Priestly and his associates, Jesus was able to perform miracles, a supernatural power which was undoubtedly given to him by God. In short, Unitarianism and deism, although having a great deal in common, developed more or less independently and along different lines.

Probably the most scholarly work written against Paine was by the English Bishop of Llandaff, Richard Watson. His *Apology for the Bible* was extremely popular in America and though designed for mass consumption, it did not descend to ridicule and scurrility. Watson seemed impressed by *The Age of Reason* for, in his reply, he spoke of the " philosophical sublimity " which he found in certain portions of the work. His many quotations from the deistic book greatly stimulated its circulation—hardly what the good Bishop expected or desired. Proceeding in a manner similar to that of Paine, Watson discussed the Old Testament

the Principles, etc. (Baltimore, 1795), pp. 116, 139-40, 145; and Williams, *Age of Infidelity: In Answer to Thomas Paine's Age of Reason* (London, 1794), pp. 11-3, 17-20, 37-40, 42, 49.

[14] See chapter iv, pp. 86, 109.

book by book and pointed out that many Hebrew scholars during the Middle Ages were cognizant of Paine's contentions. Although admitting the validity of his opponent's arguments in respect to Genesis, Watson accepted the divine origin of the Hebraic accounts and declared that if he were not a Christian, he would become a Jew. He also defended the New Testament narratives concerning the miraculous conception, the genealogy of Jesus and the resurrection. In conclusion, the Anglican clergyman pleaded with God to forgive Paine for his " infidelity ".[15] A Jew, David Levi, agreed with Watson that Hebrew scholars were quite familiar with Paine's exceptions to certain Old Testament texts. The writer especially assailed the deistic representation of the Jews as an ignorant and barbarous people [16] and in his *Defence of the Old Testament,* he showed that their religious and moral principles were superior to those of other ancient peoples. Although Levi did not expect to convert Paine, he did desire " to save " people from Paine's disbelief in revelation, a disbelief which, if circulated among Jews, might prove as destructive to Judaism as it was to Christianity.[17]

Meanwhile Paine's critics were themselves being criticized in an anonymous pamphlet attributed to Palmer and entitled *The Examiners Examined: Being a Defence of the Age of Reason* (1794). The author desired to vindicate " the undaunted champion of reason, and the resolute and unconquerable enemy of tyranny, bigotry, and prejudice. . . ."

[15] R. Watson, *Apology for the Bible, in a Series of Letters to Thomas Paine's Age of Reason* (Albany, 1796), pp. 27-36, 46, 58-61, 68-83, 87, 141, 144-5, 177, 186-7.

[16] In spite of their professed tolerance, some deists, like Morgan and Voltaire, were anti-Semites.

[17] D. Levi, *Defence of the Old Testament* (New York, 1797), pp. 5, 7, 45-9, 67-71, 119-20. It is interesting to note that copies of *The Age of Reason* have been translated into Yiddish. In 1922, one appeared in New York.

To the writer, Christianity was a monument of "ignorance and credulity, which the wisdom of the present generation probably [was] destined to overthrow. . . ." The "Examiner" not only took Williams to task for condemning Mohammedanism but even went so far as to assert that the religion of the Prophet was superior to Christianity and Judaism. He likewise condemned Ogden for his attempt to slur the character of Paine. In conclusion, the writer predicted the triumph of deism over Christianity and the substitution of "Temples of reason . . . [for] temples of superstition. . . ." [18] *The Examiners Examined* was immediately answered by a Newport clergyman, William Patten. Representing his opponent as a "Deluded worm", the preacher foretold the victory of Christianity over its enemies because its case was defended by "the perpetual care and irresistible power of God. . . ." Patten assailed the position of his deistic rival on such matters as the sufficiency of reason, the doctrine of original sin and the superiority of Mohammedanism.[19] *The Age of Reason* was assailed not only in pamphlets but also in periodicals. Paine was described in the newspapers as vain, ignorant, bold, superficial and unoriginal,[20] while his opponents received favorable consideration.[21] Magazines likewise ridiculed the advocate

[18] *Examiners Examined, etc.* (New York, 1794), pp. 6, 16, 53-60, 81, 83.

[19] W. Patten, *Christianity the True Theology . . . With an Appendix in Answer to the 'Examiners Examined'* (Warren, 1795), pp. 132-174.

[20] *Western Star*, September 9, 1794 (no. 250); *Massachusetts Spy*, October 8, 1794 (no. 1122); *The Independent Chronicle and Universal Advertiser*, December 15, 1794 (xxvi, no. 1436); *The Salem Gazette*, September 6, 1796 (no. 531); and *The Columbian Sentinel*, December 23, 1797 (no. 1436).

[21] *Massachusetts Spy*, November 19, 1794 (no. 1128), August 31, 1796 (no. 1220); *The Mercury*, December 30, 1794–January 12, 1795 (no. 235); *The Independent Chronicle*, January 12, 1795 (xxvii, no. 1445); *The Salem Gazette*, February 3 and 10, 1795 (nos. 434 and 435), August 12, 1796 (no. 524); and the *Federal Gazette and Baltimore Advertiser*, October 14, 1796 (v, no. 918).

of deism [22] and warned their readers not to peruse his work.

In the meantime, monthly publications were assailing Paine's deistic associates. In *The American Museum: or Repository* for September 1792, " Philagathos " took his skeptical adversaries to task for abusing the clergy. If unbelievers desired to popularize their views, they should republish " a new edition of Tindal-Toland-Chubb or some other of the fraternity . . ." whose works were " now out of print as well as out of credit. . . ." The writer concluded by taunting the deists with their lack of courage. Other magazine contributors defended Christianity by showing the insufficiency of deism. One author asserted that whereas natural religion was unable to explain the creation of the world and the origin of sin, the Christian revelation was capable of doing so.[23] Another writer, in *The South-Carolina Weekly Museum* for January 1, 1797, asserted the inability of deism to establish solidly the idea of immortality because such a principle could not be proved by " natural deductions and unassisted reason. . . ." Unable to offer any definite hope of salvation, deism was worthless in the hour of death. For the edification of those deists who still hoped to achieve heaven, *The Connecticut Evangelical Magazine* for March 1801 told how a freethinker, steeped in the militant deistic teachings of Allen, Paine and Voltaire, was forced to renounce his shallow views when faced with death. Maintaining that deism was essentially superficial, two authors, one in *The Theological Magazine* for October, November and December 1797, and the other in *The Connecticut Evangelical Magazine* for October 1800, urged that

[22] *American Monthly Review*, January, 1795, vol. i, pp. 17-21; *The Theological Magazine*, January and February, 1796, vol. i, pp. 285-7; and the *Connecticut Evangelical Magazine*, July, 1801, vol. ii, p. 29.

[23] *The Rural Magazine: or Vermont Repository*, June, 1795, p. 295.

it be replaced by the divine revelation of Christianity. The young were especially advised to shun vice and infidelity in order to live happily and temperately.[24]   One correspondent, in *The Baltimore Weekly Magazine* for February 16, 1801, went so far as to assert that " every man who endeavors to invalidate the truth of the everlasting Gospel is a liar. . . ." Less hot-headed than this last contributor were others who sought to vindicate their belief in Christianity by proving the validity of its doctrines and evidences.   In 1797, a New York periodical upheld the Trinitarian creed and severely condemned Paine for his unenthusiastic acceptance of immortality.[25]

During the same year, *The American Universal Magazine* reprinted an extract from one of Dr. Price's dissertations in which the noted Englishman requested people to judge Christianity solely by the good it had done.   In 1800, *The Monthly Magazine and American Review* published a very favorable criticism of Dobson's *Letters on the Existence and Character of the Deity*.   Dobson was a Philadelphia printer and bookseller who sought to impress upon the youth of the land the truth of Christian dogmas and testimonies.   Consequently, his *Letters* defended the authenticity of the Old Testament and the need of such theological doctrines as original sin and election.   He was described by the reviewer as a " public-spirited and useful citizen . . ." who wrote like " a serious, well-informed and sensible man. . . ." [26]

The defenders of the faith also used the newspapers to

[24] *The Connecticut Evangelical Magazine*, November, 1800, vol. i, p. 197.

[25] *The Theological Magazine*, August and September, 1797, vol. ii, pp. 422-4, 429-35.

[26] For a criticism of the first part of Dobson's pamphlet consult *The Monthly Magazine and American Review*, September, 1800, vol. iii, pp. 197-200.   See also *The American Review and Literary Journal*, April, May and June, 1802, vol. ii, pp. 216-9.

spread anti-deistic arguments. Under the pretentious title, "Moral and Divine Philosophy", an anonymous writer for a Boston journal showed that Christianity consisted not only of the religion of nature but also of "matters of pure revelation." The miracles of Jesus proved the divine origin of the Christian religion which was destined to stand the test of time in spite of "all the artful, unfair and flattering opposition that has been made to it by Deists. . . ." [27] Another newspaper correspondent, "Common Sense", wrote a series of articles for *The Virginia Gazette and Richmond Chronicle* in which he defended the miracles attributed to Moses and Jesus, though he denied those credited to Mohammed. During the course of his work, the orthodox advocate was assailed by a deist who contended that the books ascribed to Moses were once lost and that Ezra had actually altered them. The skeptic was soon answered by another defender of the faith who was surprised that the remarks of "Common Sense" "should have raised the bristles of one of your Richmond Deists. . . ." Apparently "the bristles" of more than one Richmond deist had been raised as was evidenced by the fact that another freethinker severely censured "Common Sense" for misrepresenting the position of his deistic rival.[28] A Hudson newspaper likewise published a series of articles designed to prove the validity of the Biblical revelation, especially its story of the Deluge. The existing marks made by the flood upon the earth's surface and the prevalence of pagan traditions and fables were presented as

[27] *The Boston Gazette and Weekly Republican Journal* from June 30, 1794 (no. 2074) to October 27, 1794 (no. 2091) inclusive.

[28] The first essay of "Common Sense" appeared in *The Virginia Gazette and Richmond Chronicle* for March 10, 1795 (no. 213), while the ninth and last article was published on May 5, 1795 (no. 229). See especially the issues of April 4, May 5 and 9, 1795 (nos. 223, 229, 230).

proofs of the narrative's truth. Jefferson's rejection of the story was especially objected to.[29]

To check the spread of deism, the champions of Christianity used not only press but also pulpit. Particularly prominent in this crusade were the Congregational clergy of New England who endeavored to show that freethinking was subversive of a belief in the existence of God and of a continuation of organized government. With such lofty watchwords as " For God and Country! " they sought to entangle men on the barbed wires of prejudice. The effort to identify deism with atheism was reflected in a sermon, delivered in 1798, by James Dana of New Haven. After condemning the deists for their attack upon Christianity, the clergyman asserted that too many concessions were being made to these " atheists ". The divine origin of the Bible ought to be accepted by the clergy without any more ado.[30] Some three years later, Timothy Dwight also linked deism and atheism under the general head of " infidelity ". Besides he injected into the deistic controversy, the anti-French political issue. Asserting that freethinking was characteristic of the eighteenth century, he stated that its success in America was " totally unprecedented . . ." and was undoubtedly due to enthusiasm for the French revolutionaries. Yet, he modestly reassured his hearers that New England had escaped the " dreadful bondage " of deism through the untiring work of her leaders among whom was that inconspicuous servant of the Lord, Timothy Dwight.[31] The Yale President was vigorously condemned by a deistic newspaper, *The Temple of*

[29] *The Balance and Columbian Repository*, February 1 to March 1, 1803 (nos. 5 to 9).

[30] J. Dana, *A Sermon: Preached October 17, 1798 at the Ordination of the Rev. Mr. Dan Huntington* (Lichtfield, 1799), pp. 18, 22-3.

[31] T. Dwight, *A Discourse on Some Events of the Last Century.* Delivered January 7, 1801, pp. 19, 21-2, 32, 34.

Reason for April 29, 1801, which described his sermon as a bigoted and unlearned discourse. Another New England clergyman, John Foster, attempted to check deism by showing that the movement was un-American. In his sermon, *Infidelity Exposed, and Christianity Recommended* (1802), Foster held that freethinking was characteristically European and consequently the nations across the Atlantic had more to fear from the forces of darkness than our own " favored land, happily disjoined from those degenerate and luxurious regions. . . ." Yet, the danger was even present in America where Paine was being eulogized; therefore the ever vigilant minister urged all, regardless of age or sex, to be on the watch to detect and avoid the snares of deism.[82]

The more or less rational defense of Christianity necessarily appealed to a limited minority, the educated few. Most of the people were neither capable of following anti-deistic arguments nor were they especially interested in them. Weary of endless disputation and desiring a consoling faith, the masses were ready to listen to revivalist preachers who urged them to heed the promptings of their hearts which would lead them to accept without question the divine origin of the Bible and the Messiahship of Jesus. Beginning in 1792, evangelicalism made its way from New England to western New York and Pennsylvania and, by 1801, reached its peak in Kentucky and Tennessee. Although free from " abnormal excitement " in New England, the movement was characterized by " excesses " in the region west of the Alleghanies where open meetings were conducted by ignorant and unlearned preachers who reënforced their messages by dire observations on the depravity of man. At these " ingatherings ", some " sinners " would lie on the ground, suddenly arise and begin to shriek, groan and pray, while

[82] J. Foster, *Infidelity Exposed, etc.* (Cambridge, 1802), pp. 19-20, 27, 33 (Appendix, note, iv).

others, falling into trances, would unexpectedly throw themselves down and roll about like a ball. Sometimes these neurotic activities were indulged in by as many as twenty thousand people and continued for many days. It was felt that at these meetings the Spirit of God descended upon converted sinners and disclosed to them "the glorious mysteries of the Gospel." [33]

From our viewpoint, the most significant result of the Awakening of the late eighteenth and early nineteenth centuries was the advent of a more vigorous orthodox movement designed to check the progress of deism. Missionary societies, religious periodicals, Bible associations and educational institutions rendered effective service. At the turn of the century, Connecticut, New York, Massachusetts, New Hampshire and Vermont established missions in order to spread the Gospel in the West and South. Aided financially by Female Cent Institutions, these bodies possessed well filled treasuries; by 1807, the Missionary Society of Connecticut reported a permanent fund of $15,000. In 1816, a Board of Home Missions was organized to send better informed ministers westward and thereby check indifference to religion.[34] Connected with these organizations were periodicals founded for the double purpose of reporting the successful work of missionaries and of defending revelation. *The Connecticut Evangelical Magazine* and the *New-York*

[33] L. W. Bacon, *History of American Christianity* (New York, 1897), pp. 233-45; F. G. Beardsley, *A History of American Revivals* (New York, 1904), pp. 85-107; J. M. Buckley, *A History of Methodism in the U. S.* (New York, 1896), p. 298; H. M. Jones, *America and French Culture*, pp. 388, 411-2; and R. E. Thompson, *A History of the Presbyterian Churches in the U. S.* (New York, 1895), pp. 73-4.

[34] Bacon, *op. cit.*, pp. 246-7; Sweet, *Story of Religions in America* (New York, 1930), p. 352; Newman, *History of the Baptist Churches in the U. S.* (New York, 1894), p. 385; Thompson, *op. cit.*, p. 81; and Walker, *History of the Congregational Churches in the U. S.* (New York, 1884), p. 313.

Missionary Magazine and Repository appeared in 1800. These were followed by others, the most popular of which was *The Panoplist, and Missionary Magazine United.* This periodical was conducted by a society called the Friends to Evangelical Truth which, in turn, was under the patronage of the Massachusetts, Hampshire, Maine, Berkshire and Rhode Island Missionary Societies. Attaining a circulation of seven thousand readers by 1809, *The Panoplist* assailed those who desired to sap the foundation of Christian faith and consequently its sheets were filled with articles praising Christianity and vindicating the divinity of Jesus and the authenticity of the Mosaic account in Genesis.[35] Moreover, Massachusetts Baptists had their own magazine (1803 to 1807), while the Presbyterian General Assembly issued a journal containing articles which showed the absurdities of deism and the superiority of revelation.[36]

Bible and Tract Societies were also formed to fight the deistic " legions of darkness ". Securing eager volunteers from the laity and clergy of all denominations, these organizations, " convinced of the great value of the revealed will of God ", were established in Pennsylvania, Vermont, Connecticut and Massachusetts. In 1816, a national organization, The American Bible Society, appeared which immediately published copies of the Scriptures and distributed them free of charge to the farmers of the South and West. In addition to these agencies, educational institutions were founded. From 1808 to 1827, Congregationalists, Presbyterians and Episcopalians established divinity schools designed to pro-

[35] *Panoplist, and Missionary Magazine United,* June, 1808, vol. i, pp. 24-8 and October, 1808 to August, 1809, vol. i, pp. 211 *et seq.* and 391 *et seq.*

[36] *The General Assembly's Missionary Magazine; or Evangelical Intelligencer,* March, 1805 (no. 3), vol. i, pp. 133-5 and May, 1805 (no. 5), vol. i, p. 228.

duce an educated ministry which would be better prepared to meet skeptical contentions. The faithful concerned themselves not only with higher but also with lower branches of education. In order to impress upon young minds the need of the Christian religion, infant schools were founded where simple Biblical questions were answered, Scriptural scenes shown and the Ten Commandments taught. In addition, there were Sunday schools where catechisms were used. These categorically praised the truth and excellence of Christianity and condemned the falsity and absurdity of Mohammedanism.[37]

Thus, during the early nineteenth century, the forces of deism were compelled to give way before the advancing columns of evangelical Christianity. The deistic army, though eventually defeated, was far from routed. In the ' twenties and early 'thirties, it reformed its wavering ranks and renewed its attack under the banners of Utopian socialism. Frances Wright and the Owens endeavored to liberate the proletariat from " the opium of religion " but all to no avail. In the end, " the foot of the spoiler " was unable to " trample down the cross of the redeemer ". Even though militant deism was unable to accomplish this objective, it nevertheless profoundly affected American intellectuals. The Higher Criticism, which sought to determine after careful investigation the authorship and dates of Scriptural books and passages, was influenced by it. This tendency, which originated in Germany, made its way to America during the early nineteenth century [38] and was popularized here by Thomas Cooper, President of the College of

---

[37] See *A Missionary Catechism for the Use of Children* published by the Yale College Society of Inquiry concerning Missions (New Haven, 1821), pp. 6, 8-12.

[38] John Adams mentioned it in a letter to Jefferson ,July 18, 1813. Wilstach, *Correspondence of John Adams and Thomas Jefferson*, p. 69.

South Carolina and Theodore Parker, Unitarian minister.[39] Although many deistic observations on the Bible were superficial and biased, some, especially on the Pentateuch, were penetrating and later verified.

The New England Unitarian movement of the nineteenth century had something in common with the deistic tendency; both agreed as to the attributes of God, the aim of religion and the character of Jesus. William Channing, a leading Unitarian, accepted the deistic notion that the Supreme Being was so benevolent and just that He would not damn the greater part of mankind for the sake of a chosen few. Moreover, as with most deists, so with Channing, the end of religion was the love of God and the practice of the good life. Furthermore, the New England clergyman in describing Christ as a tender, humble and philanthropic soul distinct from and inferior to God was merely stating what the disciples of deism were saying all along.[40] Yet, a wide gulf separated Channing and the deists and that gulf was revelation and miracles. Unlike the deistic champions, he argued that Christian " disclosures " were needed to make " the voice of nature " more audible and that supernatural acts in general and those of Jesus in particular were of divine origin.[44] In short, the Unitarianism of Channing was more than a diluted form of deism purged of its anti-Christian ingredients. Developing along different lines the Unitarian

---

[39] See Cooper, *A Letter to Prof. Silliman On the Connection between Geology and the Pentateuch* (Boston, 1833), pp. 21-2, 31-2, 39-40, 47-8 and Parker, *A Discourse on the Transient and Permanent in Christianity* (Boston, 1841), pp. 21-2. Consult also Parrington, *Main Currents in American Thought*, vol. ii, pp. 417-8 and Robertson, *Short History of Free Thought*, vol. ii, p. 438.

[40] Channing, *A Sermon, Delivered at the Ordination of the Rev. Jared Sparks* (Liverpool, 1821), pp. 18-9, 23, 25, 31 and *Works* (Boston, 1875), pp. 228-9, 385.

[41] Channing, *Works*, pp. 221, 223-4, 230, 232, 384.

movement was essentially hostile to it.   Uncompromising in the eighteenth century, it remained so in the nineteenth when " infidelity " was only a hollow shell.   Proposing to stamp it out by discarding traditional Calvinistic doctrines and by interpreting the Bible along " reasonable " lines, Channing employed arguments reminiscent of the liberal and dignified apologists of the eighteenth century.   It is interesting to note that long after deism had died out as an independent movement, a transcendental Unitarian.   Theodore Parker went beyond Channing's position by rejecting the Biblical revelation and the miracles of Christianity and substituting for them " the absolute Religion of Nature" consisting of " normal feelings toward God and man, of the correct thoughts about God and man, and the relation between them, and of actions corresponding to the natural conscience. . . ." [42]

[42] T. Parker, *A Discourse on the Transient and Permanent in Christianity*, p. 19 and Weiss, *The Life and Correspondence of Theodore Parker* (New York, 1864), vol. ii, pp. 451-2, 464, 474 (Appendix).

LIST OF AUTHORITIES

The works cited below are arranged under the various chapter headings

EUROPEAN BACKGROUND

PRIMARY SOURCES

Blount, C., *Oracles of Reason* (London, 1693).

Bolingbroke, H. St. John, *Works*, ed. D. Mallet (London, 1754).

Cheyne, G., *Philosophical Principles of Religion: Natural and Revealed* (London, 1715).

Chubb, T., *True Gospel of Jesus Christ Asserted. To which is added a Short Dissertation on Providence* (London, 1738).

Clarke, S., *A Discourse concerning the unchangeable Obligations of Natural Religion, and the Truth and Certainty of the Christian Revelation* (in Watson, R., *A Collection of Theological Tracts* [London, 1791], vol. iv, pp. 109-295).

——, *Discourse on Natural Religion* (in Selby-Bigge, L. A. [ed.], *British Moralists, Being Selections from Writers Principally of the Eighteenth Century* [Oxford, 1897], vol. ii, pp. 3-56).

Collins, A., *A Discourse of Free-thinking occasioned by the rise and growth of a sect called Free-thinkers* (London, 1713).

——, *Discourse of the Grounds and Reasons of the Christian Religion* (London, 1724).

Herbert of Cherbury, *Religion of the Gentiles with the Causes of their Errors* (London, 1705).

d'Holbach, P. H., *The System of Nature; or the Laws of the Moral and Physical World* (London, 1836).

Locke, J., *Essay Concerning Human Understanding*, ed. A. S. Fraser (Oxford, 1894).

——, *Reasonableness of Christianity. To which is added A Discourse on Miracles* (One of a volume of nine pamphlets in the Columbia University Library, no title page).

Newton, I., *Mathematical Principles of Natural Philosophy*, translated by Motte (London, 1803).

Pope, A., *Essay on Man* (in Richards, J. A. [ed.], *Outline of Knowledge* [New York, 1924], vol. xi, pp. 289-318).

Rousseau, J. J., *Confessions*, Hedouin Edition (London, no date).

——, *Emilius and Sophia; or A New System of Education* (London, 1783).

——, *Profession of Faith of A Savoyard Vicar* (New York, 1889).

179

Shaftesbury, A., *Characteristics of Men, Manners, Opinions, Times, etc.*, ed. J. M. Robertson (London, 1900).

Tillotson, J., *Works* (London, 1717).

Toland, J., *Christianity not Mysterious: or A Treatise Shewing, That there is nothing in the Gospel Contrary to Reason, Nor Above it: And that no Christian Doctrine can be properly call'd A Mystery* (London, 1696).

Voltaire, F. M. A. de, *Letters on the Christian Religion* (New York, no date).

——, *Philosophical Dictionary . . . with Notes, containing A Refutation of such Passages as are in any way exceptionable in regard to Religion* (London, 1765).

——, *Romances*, ed. Komroff (New York, 1928).

——, *Toleration and Other Essays*, tr. with an introduction by J. McCabe (New York, 1912).

Wollaston, W., *The Religion of Nature Delineated* (London, 1738).

Woolston, T., *A Discourse on the Miracles of our Saviour, in view of the Present Controversy Between Infidels and Apostates* (London, 1727).

CATALOGUES OF BOOKS

(See also citations under *Rise of Deism in Colonial America, Primary Sources, Catalogues of Books*)

Berrian, S., *A Catalogue* (New York, 1803).

Blake, W. P., *Catalogue of Books* (Boston, 1796).

Carey, Stewart and Company, *Catalogue of Books, etc.* (Philadelphia, 1791).

Caritat, H., *Catalogue Livres Français* (New York, 1799).

Catalogue of the Books Belonging to the Loganian Library (Philadelphia, 1795).

Catalogue of Books in the Massachusetts Historical Library (Boston, 1796).

The Charter, Bye-Laws, and Names of the Members of the New York Society Library: With A Catalogue of Books Belonging to the said Library (New York, 1789, 1792, 1793).

Cox and Berry, *A Catalogue of A very large Assortment of the most esteemed Books, etc.* (Boston, 1776 [?]).

Gaine, H., *Catalogue of Books* (New York, 1792).

Knox, H., *Catalogue* (Boston, 1773).

Prichard, W., *A Catalogue of a Scarce and Valuable Collection of Books* (Philadelphia, 1785).

Thomas, Andrews and Penniman, *Catalogue of Books* (Albany, 1798[?]).

PERIODICALS

(Consult citations under *Rise of Deism in Colonial America, Deism in Revolutionary America, Deism Militant* and *Christianity Defended, Primary Sources, Periodicals*)

SECONDARY AUTHORITIES

Abbey, C. J. and Overton, J. H., *The English Church in the Eighteenth Century* (London, 1878).

Benn, A. W., *History of English Rationalism in the Nineteenth Century* (London, 1906), vol. i.

Burtt, E. A., *Metaphysical Foundations of Modern Physical Science* (London, 1925).

Bury, J. B., *History of Freedom of Thought* (New York, 1913).

Farrar, A. S., *A Critical History of Free Thought in Reference to the Christian Religion* (New York, 1863).

Hunt, J., *Religious Thought in England* (London, 1870), 3 vols.

Lecky, W. E. H., *History of the Rise and Influence of the Spirit of Rationalism in Europe* (New York, 1919), vol. i.

Life of George Cheyne, M. D., with Extracts from his Works and Correspondence (Oxford, 1846).

Lodge, O., *Pioneers of Science* (London, 1893).

McGiffert, A. C., *Protestant Thought Before Kant* (New York, 1911).

Morley, J., *Rousseau* (London, 1891), vol. ii.

——, *Voltaire* (London, 1919).

Overton, J. H. and Relton, F., *English Church from the Accession of George I to the End of the Eighteenth Century* (London, 1906).

Pattison, M., *Essays*, collected and arranged by H. Nettleship (Oxford, 1889).

Randall, J. H, *The Making of the Modern Mind* (Boston, 1926).

Robertson, J. M., *Short History of Free Thought* (New York, 1906), vol. ii.

Sedgwick, W. T. and Tyler, H. W., *Short History of Science* (New York, 1923).

Shields, C. W., *The Final Philosophy* (New York, 1877).

Stephen, L., *English Thought in the Eighteenth Century* (New York, 1902), vol. i.

Whitehead, A. N., *Science and the Modern World* (New York, 1925).

RISE OF DEISM IN COLONIAL AMERICA (1713-1763)

PRIMARY SOURCES

Adams, J., *Works*, ed. C. F. Adams (Boston, 1850).

Briant, L., *The Absurdity and Blasphemy of Depretiating Moral Virtue* (Boston, 1749).

Byrd, W., *Writings*, ed. Bassett (New York, 1901).

Chauncy, C., *Benevolence of the Deity, Fairly and Impartially Considered* (Boston, 1784).

——, *Seasonable Thoughts on the State of Religion in New England* (Boston, 1743).

Clap, T., *An Essay on the Nature and Foundations of Moral Virtue and Obligations; being a Short Introduction to the Study of Ethics* (New Haven, 1765).

Colden, C., *An Explication of the First Causes of Action in Matter, and the Cause of Gravitation* (New York, 1746).

Dickinson, J., *Familiar Letters Upon A Variety of Religious Subjects* (Glasgow, 1775).

——, *The Reasonableness of Christianity, in Four Sermons* (Boston, 1732).

Edwards, J., *Works*, ed. S. L. Dwight (New York, 1830), vols. ii, iii, iv, xi.

Franklin, B., *A Dissertation on Liberty and Necessity, Pleasure and Pain* (in I. W. Riley, *American Philosophy—Early Schools* [New York, 1907], pp. 571-80).

——, *Memoirs* (New York, 1839), vol. ii.

——, *Writings*, ed. A. H. Smyth (New York, 1905-07).

——, *Works*, ed. J. Sparks (Boston, 1836).

Gay, E., *Natural Religion, As Distinguish'd From Revealed* (Boston, 1759).

Johnson, S., *An Introduction to the Study of Philosophy* (New London, 1743).

——, *His Career and Writings*, ed. H. and C. Schneider (New York, 1929).

——, *A Letter from Aristocles to Authades Concerning the Sovereignty and the Promises of God* (Boston, 1745).

Livingston, W., *Philosophic Solitude: or, The Choice of a Rural Life, A Poem* (New York, 1747).

Mather, C., *Student and Preacher; or Directions for a Candidate of the Ministry* (London, 1789).

——, *Christian Philosopher* (London, 1721).

——, *Reasonable Religion: or, the Truths of the Christian Religion Demonstrated* (London, 1713).

Mayhew, J., *Two Sermons on the Nature, Extent and Perfection of the Divine Goodness. Delivered December 9, 1762* (Boston, 1763).

Smith, W., *Discourses on Public Occasions in America* (London, 1762), Appendix, pp. 39-103, 147-60.

Wesley, J., *An Extract of the Reverend Mr. John Wesley's Journal, etc.* (Bristol, 1739 [?]).

Whitefield, G., *A Continuation of the Reverend Mr. Whitefield's Journal, etc.* (London, 1744).

Wigglesworth, E., *A Letter to the Reverend Mr. George Whitefield, by Way of A Reply to his Answer to the College Testimony against him and his Conduct* (Boston, 1745).

MANUSCRIPT MATERIAL

Hawley, J., *Confession of His Belief in Arminianism* (New York Public Library).

Johnson, S., *The Necessity of Reveal'd Religion. A Sermon . . . delivered September 7, 1727 at Stratford* (Columbia University Library).

PERIODICALS

(In these citations and in those following under *Periodicals*, dates of magazines are only given)

The American Magazine (Boston, 1743-46). Also called *The American Magazine and Historical Chronicle; for all the British Plantations.*

The American Magazine and Monthly Chronicle for the British Colonies (Philadelphia, 1757-8).

The American Weekly Mercury.

The General Magazine, and Historical Chronicle, For all the British Plantations in America (Philadelphia, 1741).

The Maryland Gazette.

The New American Magazine (Woodbridge, 1758-60).

The New-York Gazette.

The New-York Gazette Revived in the Weekly Post-Boy.

ALMANACS

Ames, N., *An Astronomical Diary, or, an Almanack for the Year of Our Lord Christ 1733* (Boston, 1733).

More, T., *The American Country Almanack, For the Year of Christian Account 1748* (New York, 1748).

Nadir, W., *Mercurius Nov-Anglicanus, or An Almanack Anno Domini 1743* (Boston, 1743).

Taylor, J., *Pennsilvania, 1743, An Almanack, or Ephemeris* (Philadelphia, 1743).

CATALOGUES OF BOOKS

Byrd, W., *Writings*, ed. J. S. Bassett (New York, 1901), pp. 413-44.

A Catalogue of Books, Imported and to be Sold by Henry Knox (Boston, 1773).

The Charter, Laws, and Catalogue of Books of the Library Company of Philadelphia (Philadelphia, 1764).

Clap, T., *A Catalogue of the Library of Yale College in New Haven* (New London, 1743).

Collections of the New York Historical Society for the Year 1880 (New York, 1881), pp. 339-63.

Johnson, S., *A Catalogue of my Library with the value* (sic) *of each Book.* August 15, 1726 (MS.), Columbia University Library.

The Library of the Late Reverend and Learned Mr. Samuel Lee, etc. (Boston, 1693).

SECONDARY AUTHORITIES

Adams, J. T., *Provincial Society, 1690-1763* (New York, 1927).

Brown, E. F., *Joseph Hawley, Colonial Radical* (New York, 1931).

Burton, J. H., *Life and Correspondence of David Hume* (Edinburgh, 1846).

Cambridge History of American Literature (New York, 1917), vol. i, chapter v.

Christie, F. A., *The Beginnings of Arminianism in New England* (Papers of American Society of Church History, 2nd Series, vol. iii).

Cook, E. C., *Literary Influences in Colonial Newspapers, 1704-1750* (New York, 1912).

Cooke, G. W., *Unitarianism in America* (Boston, 1902).

Curtis, M. M., *Outline of Philosophy in America* (in the Western Reserve University *Bulletin*, March, 1896).

Dexter, F. B., *A Selection from the Miscellaneous Historical Papers of Fifty Years* (New Haven, 1918).

Eggleston, E., *The Transit of Civilization* (New York, 1901).

Faÿ, B., *Franklin, the Apostle of Modern Times* (Boston, 1929).

Foster, F. H., *A Genetic History of the New England Theology* (Chicago, 1907).

Gewehr, W. M., *The Great Awakening in Virginia, 1740-1790* (Durham, 1930).

Greene, M. L., *Rise of Religious Liberty in Connecticut* (Boston, 1905).

History of the College of William and Mary from its Foundation, 1660, to 1874 (Richmond, 1874).

Ingraham, C. A., *A Great Colonial Executive and Scholar—Cadwallader Colden* (in *Americana*, vol. xix, Jan., 1925 to Dec., 1925, pp. 295-314).

Keep, A. B., *History of the New York Society Library, with an Introductory chapter on libraries in colonial New York, 1698-1776* (Devinne Press, 1908), pp. 3-122.

Lamberton, E. V., *Colonial Libraries of Pennsylvania* (in the *Pennsylvania Magazine of History and Biography*, vol. xlii, no. 3, pp. 193-234).

Massachusetts Historical Society, *Proceedings*, Second Series (Boston, 1896), vol. x, pp. 542-4.

Mott, F. L., *A History of American Magazines, 1741-1850* (New York, 1930).

Palfrey, J. G., *History of New England* (Boston, 1897).

Parrington, V. L., *Main Currents in American Thought* (New York, 1927), vol. i, *The Colonial Mind.*

Quincy, J., *The History of Harvard University* (Boston, 1860).

Reed, S. M., *Church and State in Massachusetts, 1691-1740* (U. of Illinois Studies in Social Sciences, vol. iii, no. 4, Dec., 1914).

Richardson, L. N., *A History of Early American Magazines, 1741-1789* (New York, 1931).

Riley, I. W., *American Philosophy—Early Schools* (New York, 1907).

Schneider, H. W., *The Puritan Mind* (New York, 1930).

Sedgwick, T., *A Memoir of the Life of William Livingston* (New York, 1833).

Sprague, W. B., *Annals of the American Pulpit* (New York, 1859).

Tiffany, C. C., *History of the Protestant Episcopal Church in the United States of America* (New York, 1895).

Trumbull, J. R., *History of Northampton, Massachusetts* (Northampton, 1902).

Walker, W., *History of the Congregational Churches in the United States* (New York, 1884).

Winsor, J. (ed.), *The Memorial History of Boston, including Suffolk County, Massachusetts, 1630-1880* (Boston, 1881), vol. ii, pp. 387-436.

Wright, T. G., *Literary Culture in Early New England, 1620-1730* (New Haven, 1920).

DEISM IN REVOLUTIONARY AMERICA (1763-1789)

PRIMARY SOURCES

Adams, S., *Writings*, ed. H. A. Cushing (New York, 1904-08), 4 vols.

Allen, E., *A Narrative of Colonel Ethan Allen's Captivity, etc.* (Philadelphia, 1779).

——, *Reason, the Only Oracle of Man; Or A Compendious System of Natural Religion* (New York, 1836).

Ames, N., *Essays, Humor, and Poems, with Notes and Comments* by S. Briggs (Cleveland, 1891).

Asbury, F., *Journal* (New York, 1831).

Bentley, W., *A Sermon, Preached at the Stone Chapel in Boston* (Boston, 1790).

——, *Diary* (Salem, 1905).

Dwight, T., *The Triumph of Infidelity: A Poem* (New York, 1788).

Hazlitt, W., *A Thanksgiving Discourse, preached at Hallowell, 15 December, 1785* (Boston, 1786).

Jefferson, T., *Writings*, ed. P. L. Ford (New York, 1892).

The Lee Papers (1754-1811), 4 vols. (New York Historical Society Collections, 1871-74).

Leland, J., *Writings*, ed. L. F. Greene (New York, 1845).

Madison, J., *Writings*, ed. G. Hunt (New York, 1900).

Massachusetts Historical Society, *Proceedings* (Boston, 1928), vol. lxi, pp. 250-1, 259-60.

Morris, G., *Life, with Selections from his Correspondence and Miscellaneous Papers*, ed. J. Sparks (Boston, 1832).

The Proceedings Relative to Calling the Conventions of 1776 and 1790 . . . The (Pennsylvania) Constitutions of 1776 and 1790 and A View of the Proceedings of the Convention of 1776, etc. (Harrisburg, 1825).

Randolph, J., *Letters to A Young Relative* (Philadelphia, 1834).

Stiles, E., *Literary Diary*, ed. F. B. Dexter (New York, 1901), 3 vols.

Washington, G., *Writings*, ed. J. Sparks (Boston, 1855).

——, *Writings*, ed. W. C. Ford (New York, 1889-92).

Webster, N., *The Peculiar Doctrines of the Gospel, Explained and Defended* (Poughkeepsie, 1809).

Winchester, E., *The Universal Restoration, etc.* (Bellows Falls, 1819).

PERIODICALS

The American Magazine (New York, 1787-8).

The American Magazine or General Repository (Philadelphia, 1769).

The American Museum, or Repository (Philadelphia, 1787-8).

The Boston Gazette and the Country Journal.

Boston Magazine (Boston, 1783-4).

The Christian's, Scholar's and Farmer's Magazine (Elizabeth-Town, 1789).

Columbian Magazine (Philadelphia, 1788).

The Connecticut Journal.

Continental Journal; and Weekly Advertiser.

The Country Journal and The Poughkeepsie Advertiser.

The Country Journal and Dutchess and Ulster County Farmer's Register.

The Gazette of the State of South Carolina.

Maryland Gazette; or the Baltimore Advertiser.

The New-Haven Gazette.

The New-Haven Gazette, and the Connecticut Magazine (New Haven, 1786).

The New-Jersey Magazine, and Monthly Advertiser (New Brunswick, 1787).

The New-York Journal or, The General Advertiser.

New-York Packet.

The Pennsylvania Gazette.

The Pennsylvania Journal; and the Weekly Advertiser.

The Pennsylvania Magazine: or American Monthly Museum (Philadelphia, 1775-6).

The Providence Gazette and Country Journal.
The South-Carolina Gazette and Country Journal.
The Worcester Magazine (Worcester, 1787).

SECONDARY AUTHORITIES

Adams, H., *John Randolph* (New York, 1899).

Adams, H. B., *College of William and Mary: A Contribution to Higher Education* (Washington, 1887).

Allen, J. H. and Eddy, R., *A History of the Unitarians and Universalists in the United States* (New York, 1894).

Bacon, L. W., *A History of American Christianity* (New York, 1901).

Beard, C. A., *An Economic Interpretation of the Constitution of the United States* (New York, 1925).

Boutell, L. H., *The Life of Roger Sherman* (Chicago, 1896).

Bruce, W. C., *John Randolph of Roanoke, 1773-1833* (New York, 1922).

Channing, E., *A History of the United States* (New York, 1924), vol. iii.

Chinard, G., *Thomas Jefferson, The Apostle of Americanism* (Boston, 1929).

Conway, M. D., *Ethan Allen's Oracles of Reason* (in the *Open Court Magazine*, January 28, 1892, vol. vi).

——, *Omitted Chapters of History Disclosed in the Life and Papers of Edmund Randolph* (New York, 1889).

Faÿ, B., *The Revolutionary Spirit in France and America*, tr. by R. Guthrie (New York, 1928).

Fiske, J., *Essays Historical and Literary* (New York, 1902), vol. i.

Foster, W. E., *Stephen Hopkins* (in the Rhode Island Historical Tracts, no. 19), [Providence, 1884]).

Garland, H. A., *Life of John Randolph of Roanoke* (New York, 1851), vol. ii.

Haroutunian, J., *Piety versus Moralism: The Passing of the New England Theology* (New York, 1932).

Henry, W. W., *Patrick Henry, Life, Correspondence and Speeches* (New York, 1891).

Jones, H. M., *America and French Culture, 1750-1848* (Durham, 1927).

Kraus, M., *Intercolonial Aspects of American Culture* (New York, 1928).

Meade, W., *Old Churches, Ministers and Families of Virginia* (Philadelphia, 1861).

Maugras, G., *La Fin d'Une Societié, Le Duc de Lauzun et La Cour de Marie-Antoinette* (Paris, 1895).

McCabe, J., *Six Infidel Presidents* (in the *Haldeman-Julius Quarterly*, April, 1927, vol. i, no. 3, pp. 33-51).

Pell, J., *Ethan Allen* (New York, 1929).

Purcell, R. J., *Connecticut in Transition, 1775-1818* (Washington, 1918).

Randall, H. S., *The Life of Thomas Jefferson* (New York, 1858).

Rives, W. C., *History of the Life and Times of James Madison* (Boston, 1859).

Rowland, K. M., *Life of George Mason* (New York, 1892).

Sanderson, J. and Waln, R. (ed.), *Biography of the Signers To the Declaration of Independence* (Philadelphia, 1823-4, 1827).

Scudder, H. E., *Noah Webster* (Boston, 1882).

Sears, L. M., *George Washington* (New York, 1932).

Sherlock, C. C., *Tall Timbers* (Boston, 1926).

Thompson, R. E., *A History of the Presbyterian Churches in the United States* (New York, 1895).

Wallace, D. D., *Life of Henry Laurens* (New York, 1915).

George Washington, The Christian (Issued by the United States George Washington Bicentennial Commission, A. B. Hart, historian, Washington, 1931).

DEISM MILITANT: EARLY NATIONAL PERIOD (1789-1805)

PRIMARY SOURCES

Ames, F., *Works*, ed. S. Ames (Boston, 1851), vol. i.

Dwight, T., *A Discourse on Some Events of the Last Century* (New Haven, 1801).

Freneau, P., *Letters on Various Interesting and Important Subjects* (Philadelphia, 1799).

Hamilton, A., *Works*, ed. H. C. Lodge (New York, 1904).

Harris, T. M., *Constitutions of the Ancient and Honorable Fraternity of Free and Accepted Masons . . . together with a History and General Regulations of the Grand Lodge of Mass.* (Worcester, 1798).

——, *Ignorance and Prejudice shewn to be the Only Enemies To Free Masonry . . . in A Sermon* (Leominister, 1797).

Leland, J., *A Blow at the Roots: Being a Fashionable Fast Day Sermon delivered at Cheshire, April 9, 1801* (New London, 1801).

Linn, W., *Serious Considerations on the Election of a President: Addressed to the Citizens of the United States* (New York, 1800).

Marcus Brutus (pseud.), *Serious Facts, Opposed to ' Serious Considerations': or, The Voice of Warning to Religious Republicans* (New York [?] 1800).

Massachusetts Historical Society, *Collections* (Boston, 1891), 6th Series, vol. iv.

Morris, G., *Writings*, ed. J. Sparks (Boston, 1832), 3 vols.

Morse, J., *A Sermon, Exhibiting The Present Dangers, and Consequent Duties of the Citizens of the United States of America* (Charlestown, 1799).

Nelson, D., *The Cause and Cure of Infidelity, etc.* (New York, 1841).

Payson, S., *Proofs of the Real Existence, and Dangerous Tendency of Illuminism* (Charlestown, 1802).

Owen, R. and Campbell, A., *The Evidences of Christianity; A Debate* (Cincinnati, 1852).

Paine, T., *The Age of Reason, Being An Investigation of True and Fabulous Theology* (New York, no date). Willey Book Co.

——, *A Letter to the Hon. Thomas Erskine . . . with His Discourse At The Society of the Theophilanthropists* (Paris, 1797).

——, *Works*, ed. W. M. Van der Weyde (New Rochelle, 1925).

——, *Writings*, ed. M. Conway (New York, 1894-1896).

Palmer, E., *Principles of Nature; or A Development of the Moral Causes of Happiness, and Misery among the Human Species* (London, 1823).

Political Miscellany Containing . . . Extracts from an Oration, delivered by Elihu Palmer, 4 of July, 1793 (New York, 1793).

Posthumous Pieces of Elihu Palmer . . . To which are prefixed A Memoir of Mr. Palmer, by his friend John Fellows of New York, and Mr. Palmer's Principles of the Deistical Society of New York (London, 1824).

Priestley, J., *Observations on the Increase of Infidelity. To which are added Animadversions on the Writings of several Unbelievers, especially The Ruins of Mr. Volney* (Philadelphia, 1797).

Smith, W. (ed.), *Ahiman Rezon Abridged and Digested: As A Help to all that are, or would be Free and Accepted Masons* (Philadelphia, 1783).

Volney, C. F. C. de, *Answer to Doctor Priestley* (Philadelphia, 1797).

——, *The Ruins: A Survey of the Revolutions of Empires* (New York, 1796).

Williams, J., *Memoirs of the late Reverend Mr. Thomas Belsham* (London, 1833).

PERIODICALS

(See citations under *Christianity Defended* [1789-1805], *Periodicals*)

The American Mercury.

The American Review, and Literary Journal (New York, 1801-2).

The Balance and Columbian Repository.

Massachusetts Spy: or The Worcester Gazette.

The New-Harmony Gazette.

The Panoplist, and Missionary Magazine United, New Series.

The Pennsylvania Gazette.

Prospect, or View of the Moral World.

The Temple of Reason.

The Temple of Truth.

The Theological Magazine, or Synopsis of Modern Religious Sentiment (New York, 1796-9).

The Theophilanthropist; Containing Critical, Moral, Theological and Literary Essays (New York, 1810).

SECONDARY AUTHORITIES

Albert, G. D., *History of the County of Westmoreland, Pennsylvania* (Philadelphia, 1882).

Amory, T. C., *Life of James Sullivan* (Boston, 1859).

Austin, J. T., *The Life of Elbridge Gerry* (Boston, 1828).

Beard, C. A., *Economic Origins of Jeffersonian Democracy* (New York, 1915).

Clark, H. H., *Toward A Reinterpretation of Thomas Paine* (in *American Literature*, vol. v, no. 2, May, 1933, pp. 133-45).

Cleveland, G., *The Great Revival in the West, 1797-1805* (Chicago, 1916).

Fosdick, L. J., *French Blood in America* (New York, 1906).

Francis, J. W., *New York during the Last Half Century* (New York, 1857).

Gillett, E. H., *History of the Presbyterian Church in the United States of America* (Philadelphia, 1864).

Gilpatrick, D. H., *Jeffersonian Democracy in North Carolina* (New York, 1931).

Griswold, R. W., *The Republican Court* (New York, 1855).

Hamilton, J. G. de R., *William Richardson Davie: A Memoir followed by his Letters with Notes by K. P. Battle* (University of North Carolina, James Sprunt Historical Monograph, no. 7) (Chapel Hill, 1907).

Hazen, C. D., *Contemporary American Opinion of the French Revolution* (Baltimore, 1897).

Jay, W., *The Life of John Jay* (New York, 1833), 2 vols.

Koch, G. A., *Republican Religion. The American Revolution and The Cult of Reason* (New York, 1933).

Larned, E. D., *History of Windham County, Connecticut* (Worcester, 1894).

Lewis, F. and Veech, J., *The Monongahela of Old* (Pittsburgh, 1892).

McMaster, J. B. and Stone, F. D., *Pennsylvania and the Federal Constitution* (Lancaster, 1888).

Myers, E. M., *A History of the Introduction of Freemasonry and its Progress in the United States since 1732* (New York, 1900).

Nash, J. V., *Thomas Paine, Pioneer Freethinker* (in the *Haldeman-Julius Quarterly*, October, 1926, vol. i, no. 1, pp. 31-8).

Pickering, O. and Upham, C. W., *Life of Timothy Pickering* (Boston, 1867).

Robinson, W. A., *Jeffersonian Democracy in New England* (New Haven, 1916).

Ruttenber, E. M., *History of the Town of Newburgh* (Newburgh, 1859).

Scharf, J. T. and Westcott, T., *History of Philadelphia* (Philadelphia, 1884).

Stauffer, V., *New England and the Bavarian Illuminati* (New York, 1918).

Tatsch, H., *Freemasonry in the Thirteen Colonies* (New York, 1929).

Todd, C. B., *Life and Letters of Joel Barlow* (New York, 1886).

Walker, J., *Memoir of Josiah Quincy* (Massachusetts Historical Society, *Proceedings*, vol. ix [Boston, 1867]).

Westcott, T., *Life of John Fitch* (Philadelphia, 1878).

CHRISTIANITY DEFENDED: EARLY NATIONAL PERIOD (1789-1805)

PRIMARY SOURCES

Address of the Trustees of the College of New-Jersey, to the Inhabitants of the United States (Philadelphia, 1802).

Beecher, L., *Autobiography, Correspondence, etc.*, ed. C. Beecher (New York, 1864).

Channing, W. E., *A Sermon, Delivered at the Ordination of the Rev. Jared Sparks* (Liverpool, 1821).

——, *Works* (Boston, 1875).

Cooper, T., *A Letter to Prof. Silliman On the Connection Between Geology and the Pentateuch* (Boston, 1833).

Dana, J., *A Sermon, Preached October 17, 1798, at the Ordination of the Rev. Mr. Dan Huntington* (Litchfield, 1799).

Dwight, T., *The Nature, and Danger, of the Infidel Philosophy exhibited in Two Discourses* (New Haven, 1798).

——, *Travels in New-England and New-York* (London, 1823).

The Examiners Examined: Being A Defence of The Age of Reason (New York, 1794).

Fiske, N., *A Sermon Preached At The Dudleian Lecture in the Chapel of Harvard College, September 7, 1796* (Boston, 1796).

Foster, J., *Infidelity Exposed, and Christianity Recommended in A Sermon* (Cambridge, 1802).

Levi, D., *A Defence of the Old Testament, in a Series of Letters, Addressed to Thomas Paine* (New York, 1797).

A Missionary Catechism, For the Use of Children (New Haven, 1821).

Muir, J., *An Examination of the Principles contained in The Age of Reason* (Baltimore, 1795).

Nelson, D., *An Investigation of that False, Fabulous and Blasphemous Misrepresentation of Truth, Set Forth by Thomas Paine* (Lancaster, 1800).

Ogden, U., *Antidote to Deism: The Deist Unmasked; or An Ample Refutation of all the Objections of Thomas Paine* (Newark, 1795).

Parker, T., *A Discourse on the Transient and Permanent in Christianity* (Boston, 1841).

Patten, W., *Christianity The True Theology . . . With An Appendix in Answer to The Examiners Examined* (Warren, 1795).

Priestley, J., *An Answer to Mr. Paine's Age of Reason, Being a Continuation of Letters to the Philosophers and Politicians of France on the Subject of Religion; and of the Letters to a Philosophical Unbeliever* (Northumberland, 1794).

Stillman, S., *Thoughts on the French Revolution. A Sermon* (Boston, 1795).

Watson, R., *Apology for the Bible, in a Series of Letters addressed to Thomas Paine* (Albany, 1796).

Williams, T., *The Age of Infidelity: In Answer To Thomas Paine's Age of Reason* (London, 1794).

Wilstach, P. (ed.), *Correspondence of John Adams and Thomas Jefferson* (New York, 1925).

PERIODICALS

(See citations under *Deism Militant: Early National Period, Periodicals*)

The American Apollo (Boston, 1792).
American Minerva; an Evening Advertiser.
American Monthly Review (Philadelphia, 1795).
The American Moral and Sentimental Magazine (New York, 1797).
The American Museum: or Repository (Philadelphia, 1789, 1790, 1792).
The American Universal Magazine (Philadelphia, 1797).
Augusta Herald.
The Baltimore Weekly Magazine (Baltimore, 1800-1).
The Boston Gazette and Weekly Republican Journal.
The Christian's Pocket Library (New York, 1796).
The Columbian Centinel.
The Columbian Phenix and Boston Review (Boston, 1800).
The Connecticut Evangelical Magazine (Hartford, 1800-4).
Federal Gazette and Baltimore Daily Advertiser.
The General Assembly's Missionary Magazine; Or Evangelical Intelligencer (Philadelphia, 1806).
The General Magazine, and Impartial Review (Baltimore, 1798).
The Independent Chronicle and Universal Advertiser.
The Literary Museum, or Monthly Magazine (Westchester, 1797).
The Massachusetts Baptist Missionary Magazine (Boston, 1803-7).
The Mercury.
Missionary Intelligence; Being Parts of Two Reports . . . to the General Assembly of the Presbyterian Church, etc. (Philadelphia, 1813).
The Monthly Magazine, and American Review (New York, 1800).
The New Star (Concord, 1797).
The New-York Missionary Magazine, and Repository (New York, 1800-1).
The Providence Gazette and Country Journal.

The Religious Monitor, or Theological Scales (Danbury, 1798).
The Rural Magazine: or Vermont Repository (Rutland, 1795).
The Salem Gazette.
South-Carolina Weekly Museum (Charleston, 1797).
The Universal Asylum, and Columbian Magazine (Philadelphia, 1790-2).
Virginia Gazette and Richmond Chronicle.
Western Star.

SECONDARY AUTHORITIES

Bacon, L. W., *History of American Christianity* (New York, 1897).
Bangs, N., *A History of the Methodist Episcopal Church* (New York, 1892).
Battle, K. P., *History of the University of North Carolina* (Raleigh, 1907).
Beardsley, F. G., *A History of American Revivals* (New York, 1904).
Bruce, P. A., *History of the University of Virginia* (New York, 1920).
Buckley, J. M., *A History of Methodism in the United States* (New York, 1896).
Carpenter, J. E., *The Bible in the Nineteenth Century* (London, 1903).
Channing, W. H., *The Life of William Ellery Channing* (Boston, 1880).
Cooke, G. W., *Unitarianism in America* (Boston, 1902).
Davidson, R., *History of the Presbyterian Church in the State of Kentucky* (New York, 1847).
Dorchester, D., *The Problems of Religious Progress* (New York, 1881).
Goodenough, A., *The Clergy of Litchfield County* (Litchfield, 1909).
Hotchkin, J. H., *A History of the Purchase and Settlement of Western New York* (New York, 1848).
Jeyes, S. H., *The Russels of Birmingham in the French Revolution and in America 1791-1814* (London, 1911).
McGiffert, A. C., *The Rise of Modern Religious Ideas* (New York, 1921).
Newman, A. H., *A History of the Baptist Churches in the United States* (New York, 1894).
Schmidt, G. P., *The Old Time College President* (New York, 1930).
Sweet, W. W., *The Story of Religions in America* (New York, 1930).
Thompson, R. E., *History of the Presbyterian Churches in the United States* (New York, 1895).
Walker, W., *History of the Congregational Churches in the United States* (New York, 1884).
Weiss, J., *Life and Correspondence of Theodore Parker* (New York, 1864).

INDEX